THE BOOK OF JAMES
AND THE MODERN-DAY CENTURIONS

The
Book of James
and the
Modern-Day
Centurions

Bob Blanks

ISBN: 9798675104116

This book is dedicated to my wife, Evelyn, who is my best friend and was the answer to my prayers to the Lord for a good Christian woman,

to my dad, who showed my siblings and me the characteristics of Christian by his actions,

and

to my good friend Sergeant Milton S. Knight, a Tuskegee Airman who showed great perseverance, patience, and Christian love in his life in defeating the trials of hate, persecution, and apathy that he experienced in his earthly life.

Contents

Introduction

*Consider it pure joy, my brothers and sisters, whenever
you face trials of many kinds, because you know that
the testing of your faith produces perseverance.*
—James 1:2–3

Why would anyone want to be in law enforcement? Simple: it is a calling. Many of us are called to go into the lion's den and to give back to our communities out of love for our fellow man. Like the military and fire departments, we run to hazardous situations and not away from them. People say that we are crazy for doing this.

*If it seems we are crazy, it is to bring glory to God. And
if we are in our right minds, it is for your benefit.*
—2 Corinthians 5:13

Whether you work in the streets, jails, or administration, law enforcement officers face trials nearly every minute on the job. Through our trials, we are provided the opportunity to show our love for our Father through obedience to his Son, Jesus Christ. This is definitely not easy.

Our daily trials begin as soon as we leave the briefing room and are seen by the public. Whether you work on the streets or in the jails, your uniform is the first thing that identifies you as law enforcement. With ever increasing antipolice sentiment directed at us, we often are subject to verbal taunts and ridicule as soon as we are seen.

Some of the trials that we face daily are: arrogance, prejudice, taming the tongue (anger and slander), apathy, and perseverance.

If we can defeat these trials, we receive the gift of wisdom to spread the Word or evangelize while we are on earth. This wisdom provides us a glimpse into the gift of eternal life from God because of faith in Christ.

My goal in writing this book is to strengthen the faith of law enforcement so we can demonstrate our Christianity to others, whether in the station, in jail, on the streets, or at home. We have a tough job—it is much tougher that when I came on in 1982. We still have to be the on-the-spot experts in gangs, domestic violence, narcotics, mental health, child protection, crime scene investigation, and any other issue that society dumps on us. However, a few new darts have been thrown at us: terrorism, negative media via the internet, cell phone cameras, sniper attacks, organized hate groups, and betrayal by the agencies or departments that have hired us.

This book contains words and ideas given to me by the Father. The words are not my own. I hope that this book can bring some peace and comfort to those who have chosen what man has considered the most hated and reviled profession. Yet this profession that has been blessed by God via documentation in the Bible.

The five trials mentioned above are discussed in detail in the Book of James, with wisdom given to those who defeat these trials. This is why I chose this book of the Bible to focus on. The Book of James is discussed at the beginning of each chapter, with verses from other books in the Bible to support James.

Throughout the book, I'll also include some personal examples, which I call "War Stories." Most are job related, but a few are from my personal or pre-law-enforcement life.

I'll mention supervisors several times throughout this book, with me being both the supervisor and the supervised. Before I go any further, let me say that the vast majority of supervisors and managers are very good, with some being outstanding. However, the small percentage of poor supervisors creates unnecessary issues, such as low morale, distrust, and apathy toward the job. One bad apple can spoil the whole bunch. I was a deputy, sergeant, and lieutenant, so I experienced law enforcement from the vantage point of the supervised and supervisor.

I won't get into the different views or tenets of the numerous religions within the Christian faith. For the most part, I use the New Living Translation (NLT) version. I consider myself a "free agent Christian" and believe what is written in the Bible—nothing added and nothing deleted.

We are all just average people who have answered the calling to serve our community. We may never know how God has used us in serving others. For this reason, we need to continue to conduct ourselves as Christ wants us.

We don't need to be part of an organized clergy to serve others or evangelize. If this were true, then only a very few persons would ever receive the message and the ability to be saved.

As Hudson Taylor, a nineteenth-century British missionary in China, stated: "God is not looking for men of great faith, He is looking for common men to trust His great faithfulness."

CHAPTER 1

Arrogance

Now listen, you who say, "Today or tomorrow we will go to this or that city, spend a year there, carry on business and make money." Why, you do not even know what will happen tomorrow. What is your life? You are a mist that appears for a little while and then vanishes. Instead, you ought to say, "If it is the Lord's will, we will live and do this or that." As it is, you boast in your arrogant schemes. All such boasting is evil. If anyone, then, knows the good they ought to do and doesn't do it, it is sin for them.
—James 4:13–17

People associate arrogance with law enforcement, and to some degree they are correct. Some words related to arrogance are: *authoritative, dominant, uninhibited, conceited, egotistical,* and *prideful.* Based upon what our job is and what we are asked to do, we need to be authoritative, dominant, and uninhibited. We take charge of crime scenes, quell immediate physical confrontations, and temporarily take away personal freedom. We have a major impact in the lives of both victims and suspects. To be successful in emergent situations, we cannot worry that we hurt someone's feelings or be afraid to take action. We, like the military, we are the "alpha dogs."

We also meet the negative descriptors as well: *conceited, egotistical,* and *prideful.* If you notice, all six descriptors of arrogance deal with ego or self. The first three descriptors are a positive use of self, to help others. The latter three deal with negative use of self for personal pride.

In Proverbs 6, God lays out six things that he detests. The first thing listed is "haughty eyes" or arrogance. Additionally, Jesus mentions arrogance in Mark 7:22 as an evil thing that comes from within and defiles a person. Arrogance takes us away from God. It makes us number one, instead of God.

As we go through our careers, certain events will shape our viewpoints and actions. These events, coupled with any negative occurrences or events that we have experienced in our pre-law-enforcement life, can create ill will and unnecessary strife in relations between law enforcement and the public we serve. This applies to the streets and jails. We have to be careful to keep our Christian faith at the forefront and any personal sentiment in the locker room.

Authority

Per the *Oxford Dictionary, authority* is defined as "the power or right to give orders, make decisions, and enforce obedience: 'he had absolute authority over his subordinates.'"

The *Merriam-Webster Dictionary* defines *authority* as:

> 1 a: power to influence or command thought, opinion, or behavior the president's authority

> 1 b: freedom granted by one in authority: RIGHT Who gave you the authority to do as you wish?

> 2 a: persons in command specifically: GOVERNMENT the local authorities of each state.

Our authority as law enforcement comes from our superiors and governmental entities or statutes. In effect we are soldiers carrying out orders from above. In California, peace officer authority comes from the California Penal Code Sections 830-832.17, Chapter 4.5. The penal code defines who a law enforcement officer is and what authority they have.

There is not a hard and steadfast written definition of a Christian. The actual word *Christian* is only used in three places in the Bible: twice in Acts and once in 1 Peter.

This is because the word *Christian* was new at the time of writings of the books of the New Testament. Also, the word was initially an insult, given to followers of Christ by their enemies.

> *It was at Antioch that the believers were first called Christians.*
> —Acts 11:26

> *But it is no shame to suffer for being a Christian. Praise God for the privilege of being called by his name!*
> —1 Peter 4:16

> *Agrippa interrupted him. "Do you think you can persuade me to become a Christian so quickly?"*
> —Acts 26:19–28

Instead of a specific definition of a Christian, the entire documentation of Jesus's life gives us the definition of what a Christian is. Jesus is the ultimate authority, yet he knew where his authority came from, and he ceded it to the Father.

> *My message is not my own; it comes from God who sent me.*
> —John 7:16

No one can take my life from me. I sacrifice it voluntarily. For I have the authority to lay it down when I want to and also to take it up again. For this is what my Father has commanded.
—John 10:18

Prayer

Knowing that we can't obtain salvation on our own authority, Jesus used his authority to teach us how to pray and ask God for what we need. The most important example of prayer is the Lord's Prayer:

> Once Jesus was in a certain place praying. As he finished, one of his disciples came to him and said, "Lord, teach us to pray, just as John taught his disciples." Jesus said, "This is how you should pray: Father, may your name be kept holy. May your Kingdom come soon. Give us each day the food we need, and forgive us our sins, as we forgive those who sin against us. And don't let us yield to temptation." (Luke 11:1–4)

Jesus also gave us personal examples of praying and seeking God's help before making a decision:

But Jesus often withdrew to the wilderness for prayer. (Luke 5:16)

> Father, the hour has come. Glorify your Son so he can give glory back to you. For you have given him authority over everyone. He gives eternal life to each one you have given him. And this is the way to have eternal life—to know you, the only true God, and Jesus Christ, the one you sent to earth. I brought glory to you here on earth by completing the work you gave me to do. (John 17:1–4)

> He took Peter and Zebedee's two sons, James and John,
> and he became anguished and distressed. He told them,
> "My soul is crushed with grief to the point of death.
> Stay here and keep watch with me." He went on a little
> farther and bowed with his face to the ground, praying,
> "My Father! If it is possible, let this cup of suffering be
> taken away from me. Yet I want your will to be done,
> not mine." (Matt. 36:37–39)

> One day soon afterward Jesus went up on a mountain
> to pray, and he prayed to God all night. At daybreak he
> called together all of his disciples and chose twelve of
> them to be Apostles. (Luke 6:12–13)

He also used his authority in keeping his promise that he would never leave us: "No, I will not abandon you as orphans—I will come to you" (John 14:18).

Moses, Paul, and the apostles also prayed before making decisions regarding their God given authority. Moses had such authority that his father-in-law, Jethro, saw that he was exhausted and almost "burned out" in leading the Israelites. In Exodus 18, Jethro suggested that Moses assign some of his authority in solving routine or day-to-day matters to others. This freed Moses to seek God's counsel in teaching his law to the people. In allocating authority to others, Moses and Jethro created leadership delegation. Also, Moses further demonstrated good leadership by not being arrogant or micromanaging. He acted upon wise advice of Jethro, after praying to God for counsel.

The apostles, having all authority bestowed upon them by Jesus, also prayed before making major decisions. In Acts 1, the apostles asked for the Lord's guidance in finding a replacement for Judas. Matthias was chosen as the new apostle.

In Acts 6, the apostles were being overwhelmed with the daily disbursement of food. They convened with all the believers and asked the Holy Spirit's help in appointing seven disciples (including the first

Christian martyr, Stephen) to handle the daily disbursement of food so they would not be "waiting on tables."

Paul, upon receiving authority from Jesus himself, prayed constantly that he and his companions would be successful in preaching the Gospel to the Gentiles. In Galatians 1, Paul, after three years of preaching the Gospel in Arabia and Damascus, went to Jerusalem and met with Peter and James to discuss his preaching authority. In Galatians 2, he met with James, John, and Peter in Jerusalem fourteen years after his first visit.

During the second visit, Paul gave them documentation of the Gospel preached to the Gentiles. After meeting and praying with the apostles, they gave Paul and his companions the "right hand of fellowship," meaning that they agreed to Paul's preaching.

The Bible shows that Paul went to meet with the apostles and used his authority through prayer to confirm that there no discrepancies being taught about salvation through Jesus Christ. Had Paul continued preaching without meeting the apostles, two different Gospels may have been preached.

Instead, Paul wanted to ensure that there is one God for both Jews and Gentiles, and only one way to seek God—Jesus. The apostles did not seek Paul, but Paul, by the authority bestowed upon him by Jesus, followed the Holy Spirit and sought out the apostles. The results were tremendous. Christianity spread through Europe, Greece, and Asia Minor during the lifetimes of the apostles and Paul.

Paul further demonstrated his authority both before and after he became a Christian. As a Pharisee, he was a witness to the martyrdom of Stephen and asked all synagogues in Damascus for their help in arresting Christians. After his conversion, Paul used the same authoritative manner to spread the Gospel, only now he was sent by Christ and sought God's guidance via prayer. It is no coincidence that Jesus chose Paul to preach to the Gentiles after the Jews had rejected their former protégé:

> And so, King Agrippa, I obeyed that vision from
> heaven. I preached first to those in Damascus, then in
> Jerusalem and throughout all Judea, and also to the

Gentiles, that all must repent of their sins and turn
to God—and prove they have changed by the good
things they do. Some Jews arrested me in the Temple
for preaching this, and they tried to kill me. But God
has protected me right up to this present time so I can
testify to everyone, from the least to the greatest.

I teach nothing except what the prophets and Moses said
would happen—that the Messiah would suffer and be
the first to rise from the dead, and in this way announce
God's light to Jews and Gentiles alike."

Suddenly, Festus shouted, "Paul, you are insane. Too
much study has made you crazy!" But Paul replied, "I
am not insane, Most Excellent Festus.

What I am saying is the sober truth, and King Agrippa
knows about these things. I speak boldly, for I am sure
these events are all familiar to him, for they were not
done in a corner! King Agrippa, do you believe the
prophets? I know you do—"
(Acts 26:19–27)

Paul could be seen as authoritatively arrogant in his conversation
with King Agrippa. Agrippa was not looking to become a Christian.
Both he and Festus insulted Paul because of the faith in Jesus that Paul
demonstrated.

Paul was obeying the orders of Christ, much like a soldier. Paul, still
obeying the command of Christ, actually tried to convert Agrippa. He
preached that all must repent and accept God through following Christ.
Paul also reiterated the Gospel in teaching that Jesus would be the first
to suffer and rise from the dead.

Although Paul had great authority and was led by the Holy Spirit
through prayer, he did not claim perfection or seek personal glory. He

knew that salvation could only be attained by ensuring one Gospel was preached. This is like us. We continue to stumble but never quit or give up on Christ.

> *I don't mean to say that I have already achieved these things or that I have already reached perfection. But I press on to possess that perfection for which Christ Jesus first possessed me.*
> —Philippians 3:12

Sometimes it is difficult to give up or cede authority, whether it was designated to us or authorized by law or statute. When we do not ask for God's guidance or fail rely upon the gift of wisdom that he bestowed upon us through prayer, we get into trouble. This failure leads to relying solely on our human wisdom, which is folly to God.

War Stories

I was removed as site supervisor for the main criminal court in Los Angeles County and transferred to a civil courthouse as a floor sergeant. I was less than pleased when this occurred. However, I asked for strength in handling what I interpreted as a slap in the face. I tried to do the best job that I could at my new assignment, as it was not the fault of the deputies that I now worked with that I was moved. A year later, I transferred to a great job and was promoted two years after that. Again, the Lord provides in his time!

Regarding asking for guidance and ceding authority to the Lord, British evangelist George Campbell Morgan stated: "All advice which we receive from men should be tested by remitting the same to God for ratification and amendment. Men called by God to lead are always in danger of attempting to encompass more than they are able."

Our Father knows our capabilities and does not give us more that we can handle. Through the Holy Spirit, God has bestowed certain gifts upon us for his glory. We all have choices to do use the gifts that the Holy Spirit has given us and employ them in situations where God has placed us.

As God ceded authority to Jesus on earth, Jesus cedes the same authority to us to spread the Word, as long as we are servants to him. So that we don't "over-encompass" our authority or do more than what we are being asked, we need to pray for God's guidance.

> *"For my thoughts are not your thoughts, neither are your ways my ways," declares the Lord. "As the heavens are higher than the earth, so are my ways higher than your ways and my thoughts than your thoughts."*
> —Isaiah 55:8–9

> *Endure suffering along with me, as a good soldier of Christ Jesus. Soldiers don't get tied up in the affairs of civilian life, for then they cannot please the officer who enlisted them.*
> —2 Timothy 2:3–4

Doing more than what God has called us to leads to a tendency of self-glory, arrogance, and pride. Doing less than what God has called us to do leads to laziness, indifference, and apathy. Either doing more or less for our glory is evil.

In the parable of the three servants in Matthew 25, each servant was entrusted with silver, according to their ability. What they did with the silver was their choice. The good servant was given more as he did what was right. The evil servant had what was given to him taken away because he did what was wrong.

Some people have been given great gifts who use them for great gain for God (like the first servant). Some people have been given fewer gifts, but still use them for the glory of God (second servant). Others are lazy and evil and disregard the gifts from God (third servant).

Just as the master gave the three servants a lifelong career, God has given us a profession or calling. Some of us will rise in rank or position throughout our careers, and others will remain working the streets or jails for their whole careers. Officers who are like the first two servants will do what is right and will positively impact others. If they are Christians, they will no doubt bring some to Christ.

The lazy and evil servant is represented by officers who sit back and collect paychecks, with little or no care for the public we serve. They are the ones who use their position of authority for themselves. Their behavior is intentional, not a mistake of the heart. This group can range from the newest hire to the head of your department.

We've all worked around or for someone who used their authority for personal gain, whether for prestige, fame, or money. Sadly, I've known a few peers who went to prison for abusing their authority. When they joined law enforcement, they were enthusiastic and wanted to take on the world, or as I used to say, "Keep the world safe for urban democracy." However, as they were promoted or received specialized assignments, the taste of power overcame them. They became greedy and felt they were above the law. They lost their pensions and were assigned to custody—only this time, on the other side of the bars.

Authority must be accompanied by humility. The greatest example of humble authority is Jesus—the one who sits at the Right Hand of God came down to earth and became man.

> *For when you die and are buried with your ancestors, I will raise up one of your descendants, your own off-spring, and I will make his kingdom strong.*
>
> *He is the one who will build a house—a temple—for my name. And I will secure his royal throne forever. I will be his father, and he will be my son.*
> —2 Samuel 7:12–14

> *All right then, the Lord himself will give you the sign. Look! The virgin will conceive a child! She will give*

birth to a son and will call him Immanuel (which means "God is with us").
—Isaiah 7:14

He will not fight or shout or raise his voice in public. He will not crush the weakest reed or put out a flickering candle. Finally, he will cause justice to be victorious.
—Matthew 12:19–20

You know the generous grace of our Lord Jesus Christ. Though he was rich, yet for your sakes he became poor, so that by his poverty he could make you rich.
—2 Corinthians 8:9

What we do see is Jesus, who for a little while was given a position "a little lower than the angels"; and because he suffered death for us, he is now "crowned with glory and honor." Yes, by God's grace, Jesus tasted death for everyone.
—Hebrews 2:9

Dominance

Per the *Oxford Dictionary*, the word *dominant* is defined as "stronger, and having more power and influence than other things or people."

The *Merriam-Webster Dictionary* defines *authority* as

1a: commanding, controlling, or prevailing over all others

b: very important, powerful, or successful, a dominant theme, a dominant industry, the team's dominant performance

In all critical or emergent situations, someone has to be dominant and take command. If we leave a situation to solve itself, then chaos ensues. In England, at the beginning of World War II, no one wanted to take control the oncoming Nazi menace. The prevailing thought was appeasement: to let Hitler have his Germanic ancestral grounds. This caused great panic among the British government, as no one could decide what the correct course of action should be to protect and save Great Britain. Through God's design, Winston Churchill became prime minister and took charge of his country.

With God's intervention, Churchill was able to rally his nation and held off the Nazis with limited military resources and some brilliant nonmilitary trickery. This had to be God's plan, as Churchill was a proclaimed agnostic, a boisterous alcoholic, and an egoistic man.

Great Britain nearly fell, but instead survived and held off Germany alone until the United States entered the war. In a modern example of God's power, Churchill was used by God to defeat Hitler, the man who was trying to exterminate the Jews, God's chosen people.

Hitler and Stalin (our ally at the time) wanted glory for themselves, not for their countries and definitely not for God. If you look at movies or pictures during this time, you see huge banners with the pictures of these two dictators hanging from buildings. Both had religious upbringings: Hitler was Catholic and Stalin was Orthodox. Both renounced God, opting for human ideologies. They both failed, Hitler (with Nazism) first and Stalin (with Communism) later. Satan's plan to eradicate the Jews via Hitler failed and resulted in God's people returning to the Holy Land and in the creation of modern Israel in 1948.

This is much like God's use of Pharaoh in Exodus 5–10, where God destroyed Pharaoh over his treatment of the Hebrews in order to demonstrate his power and glory, leading his people to the Promised Land: Israel.

Command

The Bible also has many stories and instances of dominance or persons taking command, both for the glory of God and for those who seek self-gain. Other than our Lord Jesus Christ, a few persons immediately come to mind in using their command for the glory of God: Joseph and Moses in the Old Testament, and Peter and Paul in the New Testament.

Joseph was the sold into slavery by his brothers out of hate. Once in Egypt, Joseph found favor with Pharaoh because of the gift of interpreting dreams bestowed upon him by God. Because of God's gift, Joseph, the former Israelite slave, became the most dominant figure in Egypt, second in command only to Pharaoh.

By following God, Joseph ended up controlling all of Egypt during the seven years of drought by selling grain that he had stored in the seven years of plenty preceding the drought. Joseph also saved his father, Jacob, and his brothers when they went to Egypt to get food during the drought.

Joseph was not angry with his brothers, as he understood that he was part of God's plan to save lives during the drought. Joseph saved Israel and the twelve tribes, including Judah, of which Jesus was to be born.

About three hundred years after Joseph came Moses. Moses was a Hebrew who was rescued as a baby and raised in luxury as the adopted son of Pharaoh's daughter. Choosing his Hebrew heritage over his Egyptian upbringing, he killed a slave master who had killed an Israelite. In what would become part of his later life, the Hebrews chastised and rebuked him. As a result, Moses fled Egypt and was approached and appointed by God to bring the Jews out of Egypt.

Reluctantly, Moses did what the Lord commanded him to do, from the time of the Burning Bush until his death on Mount Nebo, where he saw the Promised Land. Even after God denied Moses entry into the Promised Land for his failure to obey him regarding striking the rock for water, Moses continued to obey God's commands.

Having been given authority over God's chosen people, Moses documented God's commands via the Covenant Code in Exodus, as well as the books of Leviticus, Numbers, and Deuteronomy. These books contained the covenant law that Israel was to follow, until God established a new covenant through Jesus.

Peter was a fisherman, just a regular guy. He was the first of the apostles to state that Jesus was the Messiah, for which Jesus said he was provided this knowledge from God. Jesus gave Peter the "keys to the kingdom," which meant that Jesus gave Peter the authority "keys" to preach the Gospel "kingdom."

Since God gave Peter the knowledge that Jesus was the Messiah, Jesus had great trust in Peter. Christ knew that Peter would continue the preaching of the Gospel as directed by God, so what Peter allowed, Christ allowed, and what Peter disavowed, Christ disavowed. Amazing! Imagine the Messiah giving this dominance or control to an average Joe.

After the Ascension, Peter continued as handler of the "keys to the kingdom." He led the apostles in spreading the Good News. His dominance, or leadership, among the apostles has been documented in all four Gospels, as well as the book of Acts.

The Bible documented the change in Peter's life from a man with a hot temper and limited learning to a man of great patience and God-inspired knowledge because of his faith in Jesus Christ.

As Peter became the apostle to the Jews, Paul became the apostle to the Gentiles. God had all bases covered. Paul was a Jew trained by Gamaliel, a highly respected Pharisee doctor of Jewish law. In Acts 5, Gamaliel spoke to the High Council after the apostles were arrested for preaching about Jesus. Gamaliel recommended that the apostles not be killed, as if their message was from God; then the High Council would be fighting God. Due to Gamaliel's reputation and position, the High Council took his advice.

In Acts 22, Paul cites his education under Gamaliel when giving his testimony about his prior life in Judaism. This gave Paul immediate credibility with the accusing Jews who wanted to kill him. The use of Gamaliel to save the apostles and later to give Paul standing with the Jews is an example of God's brilliant plan to bring salvation to us.

After Paul's conversion, he suffered greatly. In 2 Corinthians, he describes the trials and pain that he experienced as he preached Christ to the Gentiles. Throughout his ordeals, he remained faithful to God and provided commands to Christians via his letters. His commands were never for self-glory, but for the glory of God through Jesus. His selflessness, sense of duty, and command are great ideals for law enforcement to strive for.

The fact that Paul was a Pharisee and persecuted Christians before meeting Christ proves that we, too, will be forgiven from our prior lives before accepting Christ.

In looking at these four men of the Bible, I found it very interesting that Satan fought with Michael over the body of Moses and asked Jesus for Peter. Satan knew that these two men were dominant and critical in the preaching of God's word, Moses in the Old Testament and Peter in the New Testament. Satan is not a fool. I'm sure he thought if he could get to these two pillars of God, the he might have a chance to overthrow God. It didn't happen and never will!

> *But for twenty-one days the spirit prince of the kingdom of Persia blocked my way. Then Michael, one of the archangels, came to help me, and I left him there with the spirit prince of the kingdom of Persia.*
> —Daniel 10:13

> *But even Michael, one of the mightiest of the angels, did not dare accuse the devil of blasphemy, but simply said, "The Lord rebuke you!"* [This took place when Michael was arguing with the devil about Moses's body.]
> —Jude 1:9

> *Simon, Simon, Satan has asked to sift each of you like wheat.*
> —Luke 22:31

As there are examples in the Bible of people using their dominance or command for the glory of God, there is no shortage of persons using this for their own glory.

Ahab and Jezebel were killed as a result of their evil ways. No king was as evil as Ahab (1 Kings 16: 33). Elijah predicted Jezebel's death in 1 Kings 21. She was thrown from a tower, her body crushed by horses, and dogs ate her flesh (2 Kings 9). In Revelation, Jesus compares the Church at Thyatira to Jezebel.

Jehorham was king of Judah and evil. He died from a painful intestinal disease that caused his bowels to spill out. He was not given a proper burial (2 Chron. 21:18–19).

Judas Iscariot betrayed Jesus and ended up hanging himself (Acts 1:18). This was predicted in Zechariah 12:12–13.

Ananais and Sapphira died after lying to Peter about the amount of money they donated to the church for property they sold (Acts 5:1–10).

King Herod was eaten by worms when he refused to give God glory (Acts 12:21–23).

In summary, God gives life to those who use the gifts given to them for his glory. Those who use their gifts for personal gain receive death.

Pride

Arrogance, boasting, and pride all go hand in hand when we tout ourselves. We forget where our accomplishments have come from and who bestowed them upon us. Becoming a peace officer places you are in a very select group. But don't let your success cloud your thinking or make you arrogant. Remember, you were placed in your position by God for a reason.

> *All who fear the Lord will hate evil. Therefore, I hate*
> *pride and arrogance, corruption and perverse speech.*
> —Proverbs 8:13

*What do you have that God hasn't given you? And if
everything you have is from God, why boast as though
it were not a gift?*
—1 Corinthians 4:7

*Believers in humble circumstances ought to take pride
in their high position. But the rich should take pride
in their humiliation—since they will pass away like a
wild flower. For the sun rises with scorching heat and
withers the plant; its blossom falls and its beauty is destroyed. In the same way, the rich will fade away even
while they go about their business.*
—James 1:9–11

*When pride comes, then comes disgrace, but with hu-
mility comes wisdom.*
—Proverbs 11:2

*For everything in the world—the lust of the flesh, the
lust of the eyes, and the pride of life—comes not from
the Father but from the world.*
—1 John 2:16

Billy Graham has a good quote regarding humbleness and pride:
"Tears shed for self are tears of weakness, but tears shed for others are
a sign of strength."

War Stories

There was a newly promoted captain who was in charge of the main jail,
which at the time housed between six thousand and seven thousand male
inmates. Wanting to make his own mark on this command, he bypassed
departmental protocol of allowing sergeants to handpick young deputies
whom they wanted to work with and train. Instead, bonus or supervising

line deputies (with whom the captain had worked the streets) were allowed to pick which new deputies they wanted to supervise. The supervising line deputies, like the captain, created their own personal cliques with forced personal loyalty.

Normally, new deputies work with general population inmates in order to become familiar jail procedures and are closely monitored by supervisors. However, these young, inexperienced deputies were assigned by the supervising line deputy on each floor to high-power modules with hardened inmates.

When the sergeants advised the captain that the results would be disastrous, the captain told them it was his jail and he would run it the way he wanted. Additionally, the captain removed some of the department-authorized authority of supervision from these sergeants and gave it to the supervising line deputy on each floor. The new deputies were not closely monitored by the supervising line deputy.

The results were worse than disastrous! Force incidents went through the roof. The ACLU become involved, and an FBI probe was initiated which had dire consequences for the department. A force incident is generally regarded as an event that requires any physical intervention by law enforcement greater than simple handcuffing or a firm grasp to restrain a suspect.

When the captain's supervisor (commander) disciplined him, he told the commander who did not report to him. The captain told the commander that he reported to, an assistant sheriff who was not responsible for custody and not in the captain's chain of command. When the commander spoke to the assistant sheriff, the assistant sheriff backed the captain and negated any supervisorial authority that the commander had. Also, the supervising line deputies did not acknowledge the authority of their supervising sergeants and lieutenants, going directly to the captain.

The captain modeled the prideful behavior of the assistant sheriff, with the supervising deputies modeling the behavior of the captain. The assistant sheriff and captain acted in a conceited, egotistical, and prideful manner, failing to act as a responsible leader of the department. Their desire of personal glory caused the entire department much pain and shame.

As a result of this incident and the ensuing FBI probe, the captain was demoted to lieutenant. However, the sheriff, assistant sheriff, and six other departmental members were sentenced to federal prison—including two friends of mine. The department, once the most respected and professional law enforcement agency in the country, was in ruins.

> *She glorified herself and lived in luxury, so match it*
> *now with torment and sorrow. She boasted in her heart,*
> *"I am queen on my throne. I am no helpless widow, and*
> *I have no reason to mourn."*
> —Revelation 18:7

Pride also leads to a manipulation of our status and creates entitlement. It is difficult to be placed in a position of authority and not abuse the position. As law enforcement. we love being in charge or in control. For many of us, this is a constant struggle.

Some believe that the uniform gives us the right to certain things that persons not in law enforcement are not entitled to. This entitlement is often the misappropriation of items entrusted to us. This could be money, drugs, public funds, or other items of value taken during an arrest or a search warrant. There was a major scandal years ago within our narcotics bureau. Although members of this bureau were making awesome arrests, some illegally used the seized funds to purchase needed equipment. They started using some of the money on themselves, buying lavish cars and homes. After a while, they got caught, and many went to prison.

Quid pro quo occurs quite often; this is the expectation something in return for a favor. The return could include anything from sexual favors to blind loyalty. We have all seen people who were promoted or given choice assignments solely because they knew someone and not because of merit. For example, a good-looking male or female officer with very limited experience is selected over several seasoned officers to a highly specialized detective unit managed by an older supervisor. Lo and behold, the new detective and the supervisor immediately become an item.

Probably the most familiar example of sexual favor is an officer stopping an attractive woman for speeding and getting her phone number in lieu of writing her a ticket. The most egregious example that I'm aware of was committed by a former academy classmate who was assigned to a court lockup facility. He would order out female inmates to his lockup who had no case within his court building. This was done so he could have sex with them. He eventually got caught and was sent to prison. In researching this case, I found that he stood trial at the court where he was formerly assigned. He was processed through the same lockup facility—only on the other side of the bars and in a blue jumpsuit instead of a green-and-tan uniform.

An example of creating blind loyalty: A department executive wants to create a power base for themselves both inside and outside the department, and promotes only persons who will do their bidding. This did occur. The local newspaper obtained a list of people who donated money to and were promoted by the executive, who was also running for a city council within Los Angeles County.

I was sadly amazed when I saw who was on both lists. I lost respect for many of the people whom I had worked with previously.

War Stories

As a sergeant, it was brought to my attention that a deputy ordered a tow truck company to release a car belonging to a relative from storage. The car was to have been stored for thirty days because the relative was driving with no insurance. The deputy signed a release slip, gave it to his relative at the station, and told the relative to have the towing company release the car with no charges. The towing company called the desk to confirm that the fee was being waived. The watch deputy looked at the release slip and told the company not to release the car. The signing deputy did not have the authority to release the car and had signed his name in the "authorizing officer" space. This was the duty of the watch deputy, who was the authorizing officer.

The signing deputy had several high-profile relatives within the station area and felt he could do what he wanted. This was not the first time that he'd violated procedure. This time he had falsified a government document. I recommended termination. Instead, he was suspended for fifteen days and transferred to a correctional facility for the remainder of his career. The arrogance demonstrated by this officer was appalling. We are to be above the law, not breaking it.

Once a deputy gave me an overtime slip, explaining that he had ridden with the engineer on a commuter train and should be paid. After I shook my head in disbelief, I told him we ride for free in uniform with the expectation to handle any incidents that occur on the train. Then I threw him out of my office.

You adulterous people, don't you know that friendship with the world means enmity against God? Therefore, anyone who chooses to be a friend of the world becomes an enemy of God.
—James 4:4

You say, "I am allowed to do anything"—but not everything is good for you. You say, "I am allowed to do anything"—but not everything is beneficial.
—1 Corinthians 10:23

Boasting

As it is, you boast in your arrogant schemes. All such boasting is evil.
—James 4:16

When boasting is done for our own benefit, it is an act of selfishness and sin. We've all tried to one-up each other with war stories. Fishermen are famous for the stories of the one that got away. I've done both. However, many times, the braggart brings others down with their stories. Young officers often hear the bogus stories of older veteran officers and want to act out these stories to be accepted. Usually, these stories involve unethical behavior, policy violations, or illegal actions.

> *They brag about themselves with empty, foolish boasting. With an appeal to twisted sexual desires, they lure back into sin those who have barely escaped from a lifestyle of deception.*
> —2 Peter 4:18

War Stories

There was an extremely reckless deputy at a station where I was assigned. He was the only person whom I was ever afraid to get into a car with. One day before his shift, he told his partner that he was going to get involved in a shooting. He did. The shooting was justifiable but could have been prevented. No one was injured. We asked him why he did this. He told us that his training officer said that he did this, and he wanted to be like his training officer. Thank the Lord he got fired a while later and never seriously injured anyone during his tenure with my department.

I've worked with guys who bragged about devised plans for their own selfish needs. One guy was a family crimes detective, working closely with victims of spousal abuse. Working with vulnerable women, he fell to temptation. He compromised his position and began dating some of the women who were spousal abuse victims. He was found out and was demoted, instead of being fired.

Another guy was assigned at a unit that worked with at-risk kids. He starting going out with some of the mothers of the kids. He was counseled and directed to stop. He didn't. He got fired.

Still another guy befriended an elderly widow with the hopes of receiving her car when she died. She saw through his scheme, leaving her car to a distant relative.

The only reasons that these three were found out is that they boasted about their actions.

One guy was assigned to a specialized unit as a bonus deputy. He went to an out-of-state training class, swapping business cards with other officers in the class. The business card that he passed out was authentic, with correct address and phone number, except that he had promoted himself to captain. This got found out when someone in the training class called the number on the business card asked for the "captain." He was a bonus deputy, on the cusp of being promoted. He was demoted from a bonus deputy and to returned to patrol. It took him a few more years to make sergeant.

I've also seen officers go to a restaurant and tell the cashier, "We're the police. We don't pay." Others have told me that when they go a theater or other event, they just flash their badge and walk in without buying a ticket. In addition to be overtly embarrassing, this is stealing—akin to defrauding an innkeeper.

These unethical, policy-violating, and illegal actions were looked upon as acceptable by many of the deputies where these events occurred—until punishment was doled out.

> *You are so proud of yourselves, but you should be*
> *mourning in sorrow and shame. And you should remove*
> *this man from your fellowship.*
> —1 Corinthians 5:2

> *They are the kind who work their way into people's*
> *homes and win the confidence of vulnerable women*
> *who are burdened with the guilt of sin and controlled by*
> *various desires.*
> —2 Timothy 3:6

In most of the instances listed above, there was a lack of supervision—in all cases, a lack of godly supervision. We know what is right and wrong, and we know if what we do is for selfish reasons or for others as Christ directs us.

Often boasting is done to make us look good in front of others. We take credit for things we haven't done or aggrandize things that we have, demonstrating no sense of team or unity.

> *When you pray, don't be like the hypocrites who love to pray publicly on street corners and in the synagogues where everyone can see them. I tell you the truth, that is all the reward they will ever get.*
> —Matthew 6:5

War Stories

A buddy of mine was on the station patio talking to a couple of commanders who were on weekend duty. He had worked with the commanders when all three were deputies. The captain came up and interrupted the conversation, boasting about the new grill and patio roof that he had purchased for the deputies. The commanders turned to him, smiled, and continued with their conversation with my buddy.

After a few minutes, the captain told my buddy to return to the desk and started bragging about what he had done on behalf of the deputies. He was on the short list for commander. He got promoted. Whether his bragging helped or not, I don't know, but he sold himself out.

People who are sycophants, brownnosers, or yes-men are other examples of boasting or bragging for self-gain. Some people will do anything for a promotion or highly sought-after position. I call this selling your soul to the devil. They align themselves with a well-connected or powerful supervisor and do whatever it takes to obtain their self-seeking goal. Often, the yes-man and supervisor cannot stand each other, but for the purpose of pride and arrogance, they align. They both brag about their accomplishments. The yes-man brags about the accomplishments that they have done for the supervisor. The supervisor brags about the same accomplishments, only he or she takes credit for them.

War Stories

In my last assignment, I was assigned as budget lieutenant. We had just absorbed a smaller county department into the sheriff's department. I knew nothing about budgets. I went from chasing gang members in East Los Angeles to becoming a bean counter. I was assigned two teams, budget and contracts, that had never worked within the sheriff's department. The people on both teams were all civilians, not sworn. Sadly, civilians tend to be looked down upon by sworn members.

My team had developed budget programs and invoice billing procedures that their former department had failed to use. We implemented these, which were much different than the sheriff's procedures. I didn't care. I had a job to do, and my team had the answer. The results were more than tremendous. In our first year, my unit provided the sheriff's department over $9 million in revenue offset. My bosses were ecstatic. I told them that the success was due to my team of civilians, not me. My team of civilians was the best group of people that I had ever worked with. They worked *with* me, not *for* me.

My budget team leader was awesome. He taught me to handle accounts payable and receivable, how to create an accurate budget, and how to provide more service to our clients while reducing their costs. He was the ultimate team player. As my budget team leader was Filipino and persons who deal with budget issues are referred to as bean counters, I proudly consider myself a white Filipino bean counter.

My contract team leader was just the opposite. She did nothing but brag about her role as an expert in contracts. She tried to butter me up at every opportunity, then negated every directive that was implemented when I was not around. When I found this out, I reprimanded her. She was pretty high on the civilian food chain. This was the first time she had ever been reprimanded. She blew a major gasket, asking me how I dared chastise her.

She was knowledgeable but not a team player, and she was a cancer to the team. She caused me and the team great difficulties for over a year. Eventually, I reduced her authority and got her transferred. I had no time for blowhards, braggarts, and brownnosers.

When hiring people for different positions, I was always amazed at the boasting provided in either their résumé or interview. Often it was aggrandizing, but more often, it was out-and-out baloney. ~~I'm dumb but not stupid,~~ I was able to see through most of their deceptions. One instance that stands out when I interviewed a guy for my data and analysis team. He told me that he was in a math fraternity in college. When I gave him the written portion of the interview process, he couldn't add two plus two. A math fraternity, really? Did he think that I was going to hire him without any type of test of his abilities? This guy wanted the job, but to out-and-out lie is not how God will grant us what we desire.

> *A person who promises a gift but doesn't give it is like*
> *clouds and wind that bring no rain.*
> —Proverbs 25:14

When I went through interviews, I was straight up with the interviewers. I once interviewed for a vice detail sergeant position. I had over fifteen years' department service, with six as a sergeant. However, I told them I had no expertise in vice crimes but could learn quickly. They said that was no problem. Their concern was that I was lying when I told them that I spoke Spanish. I'm blonde (now gray) with blue eyes and did not look like I could speak anything other than, "Dude, where's my board?" I was raised in a primarily Hispanic city in Los Angeles County, where most of my friends or their parents spoke Spanish. I used to watch *Lucha Libre* (wrestling) on Spanish television channels. Because of my upbringing, I had a very slight Anglo accent. I can roll my *r*'s with the best of them.

The interviewers, one Hispanic and one white, were surprised when I spoke Spanish and said they thought I was lying. I told them that if I lied to them, I would be expected to perform a task that I had no idea how to do.

I said that I would be doing a disservice to my team that could result in someone getting hurt or the department embarrassed. I was offered the job, but turned it down after I learned that the position was being transferred eighty miles away from home. As a single dad, this was too far from my school-age children.

I've always believed in trying for what you want and not quitting. If you don't swing the bat, you don't get a hit. I was a sergeant for seventeen years and one of the ten longest-tenured sergeants in a ten-thousand-person department. It took me six times to make lieutenant. I wanted the promotion but learned that it was in God's time.

Boasting for God

However, there are times when boasting is acceptable, when used for God's glory.

> *But those who wish to boast should boast in this alone:*
> *that they truly know me and understand that I am the*
> *Lord who demonstrates unfailing love and who brings*
> *justice and righteousness to the earth, and that I delight*
> *in these things.*
> —Jeremiah 9:24

> *Some nations boast of their chariots and horses, but we*
> *boast in the name of the Lord our God.*
> —Psalms 20:7

> *If I must boast, I would rather boast about the things*
> *that show how weak I am.*
> —2 Corinthians 11:30

Paul boasted for God about John's vision that was documented in Revelation: "I will brag about that man, but not about myself, except to say how weak I am" (2 Cor. 12:5).

Hero

There have been times when certain people have entered my life and have taught me valuable lessons. The lessons that I learned were to strengthen areas of weakness within me.

I had a friend that I met when I was forty years old. He was about eighty at the time, although he looked and acted as if he were thirty years younger. He was a Tuskegee Airman and was working full time at the Immigration and Naturalization Center in downtown Los Angeles.

We became good friends and socialized with our spouses on numerous occasions. In our conversations, he told me of about growing up in New York City and Antigua. He also told me stories of his military service. I loved hearing his stories as a tail gunner on a B-24 bomber.

He told me of the racial garbage that he and fellow Airmen endured between the time when the unit broke up after World War ll and the military became desegregated in 1948. Several states refused to house the Airmen because of the color of their skin. However, Ohio welcomed them at the Lockbourne Air Force Base. He also told me of the berating that he received from his son during the Vietnam War for supporting the United States. He told his son that violence may win the battle but would lose the war.

He never complained about his situations. I could not fathom what he went through. My friend was an everyday man and truly made a difference to me. To successfully break down barriers, one must be better that the one holding the barrier. Jackie Robinson was like this, as was my friend. My friend knew arguing was counterproductive.

> *Timothy, guard what God has entrusted to you. Avoid godless, foolish discussions with those who oppose you with their so-called knowledge. Some people have wandered from the faith by following such foolishness. May God's grace be with you all.*
> *—1 Timothy 6:21–21*

Through him, I gained a deeper understanding of the injustices that others had endured, as well as a better understanding of my faith. My friend was also a Christian who practiced his Christianity through action and character. I boast of just knowing this man and calling him my friend.

War Stories

My trainee and I received a call about a violent mental patient. We responded to the house and saw a man running in circles, flailing about, and yelling that Satan was telling him to kill himself. We assisted paramedics and ambulance techs in strapping the man to a gurney and placed him in the ambulance in order to take him to a county mental health facility. For some reason, I was in the back of the ambulance with the man. No one else was around. My trainee was in the house completing the report. The man was still yelling that Satan wanted him to kill himself and continued to flail about as he was strapped on the gurney.

Out of the blue, I asked the man if he believed in Jesus. It just came out of my mouth. He said yes. I told him to just call on the name of Jesus, and he would calm down. He called on Christ and instantly calmed, quicker than a light switch. I had never seen anything like this. I had only read about this in the Bible. To think that I saw a miracle in the healing of this man, and that Jesus used me to accomplish this miracle, is mind-boggling! I saw this event occur one other time with a mental patient, but this first miracle continues to amaze me. This event is more amazing to me than the birth of my children or anything else I have witnessed.

Each time he said, "My grace is all you need. My power works best in weakness." So now I am glad to boast about my weaknesses, so that the power of Christ can work through me.
—2 Corinthians 12:9

Involvement in Extramarital Affairs

Arrogance can lead down some pretty dark paths to self-destruction. Sex outside of marriage is one of these paths. As human beings, we love to the attention being given.

When someone is constantly having their ego stroked by an attractive person, it is easy to fall prey. Many have fallen when their cerebral cortex moved from their head and landed between their legs.

> *Give honor to marriage, and remain faithful to one*
> *another in marriage. God will surely judge people who*
> *are immoral and those who commit adultery.*
> —Hebrews 13:4

Some people are attracted to law enforcement's position of authority as a way to gain a better life for themselves and their families. In my department, we call this "looking for a man with a dental plan." Many marriages have broken up by persons looking for a man with a dental plan. This generally occurs when the law enforcement officer is older and a younger person temporarily makes them feel young again. Usually, it is all a sham.

War Stories

There was a sergeant at a station where I was assigned who was about sixty years old, with thirty-five years of service and about to enter retirement. He got a secretary, about thirty years younger than he, pregnant. His life was immediately turned upside down. He had to pay his now ex-wife a huge portion of his pension, and he now had a baby to raise. He would have been about eighty when his kid graduated high school. How unfair to the child. He did marry the secretary; she got what she wanted. This is not the solely the fault of the secretary. It takes two to tango, and the sergeant fell prey.

Another deputy whom I worked with divorced his wife and married a much younger woman who, he met in his patrol area. Things went pretty good for about five years, but then the age gap proved detrimental. He wanted to relax at home and not go out at night. She wanted just the opposite. They split because she wanted a younger and more active partner. Although she did end up with younger guy, the deputy never divorced her. He wanted her to have his pension when he dies, which she will receive until her death. He even paid for a house for her and her live-in boyfriend. Now he just goes about life fishing and drinking beer. She got him hook, line, and sinker.

Some people have a physical attraction to law enforcement; they just want to sleep with a cop. It's like a notch on their belt. Someone young and attractive offering themselves to you is very difficult to turn down. People whom I have worked with met these "doughnut dollies" at fast-food restaurants, ice cream shops, doughnut shops, and high schools. Usually younger officers who are closer in age to the women fall for this. They have not learned the lessons of working the streets that only time and experience can provide.

As these women tend to be younger, they do not have great life experience. Often, these women get attached and stalk the officer by calling the station or his home. The officer will try to hide their affair by lying to their spouse, but more times than not, the spouse finds out. In some instances, the spouse will not divorce the officer because of the financial benefits associated with law enforcement, or because they forgive them. Rarely does cheating officer change his ways, creating more acts of betrayal with the current cheating partner or others later down the road.

Likewise, officers who feel entitled look for a notch on their patrol belt, known as a "Sam or Sally Browne", as well. They often brag to each other and compare notes about their trysts. Every so often, one of the women ends up pregnant, creating many of the problems that my sergeant endured in the paragraphs above. A few of us would ask these officers why were they cheating on their spouses. They said the trysts were just one-night stands with no consequences. We would tell them be very wary. There are always consequences; five minutes of pleasure is not worth a lifetime of misery. Some stopped, most didn't.

War Stories

I remember going to a particular off-training party. These parties celebrated a deputy completing the six-month field training program, or "coming of age" within the department.

Obviously, there was much drinking (there was at mine as well). I went with my partner—a faithful husband, good father, and a Christian. We were going to grab a beer and a sandwich on our way home after our shift. As we entered the garage to say hello, there was a line of guys and couple of girls doing things that they should not have been doing. The guys called us to go over with them. My buddy and I turned and left immediately. Almost everyone in the line was married, and most ended up divorcing later on for infidelity.

Another former partner told me that he had an affair with woman in his patrol area for seven years! When he would meet with her, he told his wife that was working overtime. His wife believed him, never checking his paycheck to see if worked overtime. This was in the days of paper payroll checks, before direct deposit.

One day in the locker room, he told me that his wife was talking with someone in a chat room online. He was upset at the thought that she might be having an affair. As I looked at his locker door dotted with photos of several women whom he had met in chat rooms from across the country, I asked him, "Why is it OK for you to talk to women on line, but not your wife?" He shut up and never brought up the issue regarding his wife again. Their marriage did eventually end, after he got caught in another relationship that had lasted over five years. He was a good friend, but after his marriage ended, we drifted apart.

A young deputy met a young woman on a call. He was married; she wasn't. After work, he went to her home.

The deputy told her that he was checking on her safety, but after a while, it was apparent what the real motive was. She said that she wasn't interested. He left. There was no physical contact. She called the station and told them of the deputy's behavior. A sergeant responded and spoke to her.

A few days later, the deputy was interviewed by internal affairs (IA). The IA sergeant asked him if he went inside the woman's home. He said no. The investigator asked him again if he even went to the woman's home. He said no. The investigator asked the deputy if there was a glass in the woman's home that would have his fingerprints on it. The deputy again said no. Turned out, the deputy had a glass of water at the woman's home.

The investigator could not come out and say what evidence he had, but he gave they deputy every chance to admit that he was at the woman's home. Had he answered yes to any of the investigator's questions, he would have received a two- or three-day suspension at the most. Instead, he was fired for lying. He did not want his wife to know that he was at the woman's home.

Although infidelity among law enforcement is high, the divorce rate of law enforcement nationwide is lower than the national average. In a 2010 study conducted by Radford University in Virginia[1], the five jobs with the highest rates of divorce are machine setters, casino workers, massage therapists, dancers, and choreographers. The national average for divorce across all occupations was 16.35 percent, compared to 14.47 percent for those in law enforcement careers. The data included a divorce rate of 15.01 percent for police and patrol officers, as opposed to just over 12 percent for detectives and police supervisors.

My guess as to why the divorce rate is not higher is that the law enforcement officer is able to hide the affair(s) from their trusting spouse. Telling your spouse that you had to work late, were mandated to work overtime, or had to go on a multiday training seminar are common lies used to cover up the affair.

In my experience, younger officers brag about their cheating, while older officers are quiet as church mice. When in conversation with officers and they would tell me about their "play wife," or "boy toy," I would ask them what would their spouse think. They would say that the spouse will never know.

One thing is that they never brought up their cheating ways with me again. I'm no angel, but cheating on your spouse is lying to God. When you marry, you make a promise to him to forsake all others and keep the marriage bed pure.

The trial of infidelity is a hard one to beat, for both men and women. Infidelity within law enforcement usually begins by arrogance or entitlement. There are websites that advocate cheating on your spouse. Movies, books, and television encourage having sex out of marriage. Society mocks those who prefer chastity.

I fell prey to sex out of marriage. I was a virgin when I met my ex-wife and remained faithful throughout the marriage, but I was not after we divorced. But as I strengthened my walk with the Lord and truly placed my trust in him, I defeated infidelity. I can attest to this, as the Lord brought a Christian woman into my life. We have been blessed with a strong marriage for over fifteen years, calling upon the Lord for strength whenever issues arise.

God's Way

Through his authority from God, Jesus gave us the way to gain (not earn) eternal life or an eternal pension. We need to live life his way, as written in the Bible, and not our way. Our way is for us alone and arrogant.

> *Your Majesty, the Most High God gave sovereignty, majesty, glory, and honor to your predecessor, Nebuchadnezzar. He made him so great that people of all races and nations and languages trembled before him in fear. He killed those he wanted to kill and spared those he wanted to spare. He honored those he wanted to honor and disgraced those he wanted to disgrace.*
>
> *But when his heart and mind were puffed up with arrogance, he was brought down from his royal throne and stripped of his glory.*

He was driven from human society. He was given the mind of a wild animal, and he lived among the wild donkeys. He ate grass like a cow, and he was drenched with the dew of heaven, until he learned that the Most High God rules over the kingdoms of the world and appoints anyone he desires to rule over them.
—Daniel 5:18–21

And what do you benefit if you gain the whole world but lose your own soul?

Is anything worth more than your soul?
—Mark 8:36–37

Satan provides us an example of what happens when arrogance, boasting, or pride take over. Remember that Satan continually boasted out of pride and was cast out of heaven and ultimately will be sent to hell. Although we have the example of Satan, many of us still fall to these trials—yours truly included.

CHAPTER 2

Prejudice

*My dear brothers and sisters, how can you claim to
have faith in our glorious Lord Jesus Christ if you favor
some people over others? For example, suppose someone comes into your meeting dressed in fancy clothes
and expensive jewelry, and another comes in who is
poor and dressed in dirty clothes. If you give special
attention and a good seat to the rich person, but you
say to the poor one, "You can stand over there, or else
sit on the floor"—well, doesn't this discrimination show
that your judgments are guided by evil motives?*
—James 2:1–4

Part of our training in law enforcement is to look for illegal activity
and stop it, wherever we are assigned. This requires being proactive
and learning the high-crime areas and where the players in your patrol
area or inmate leaders ("shot callers") in your jail are. Street cops know
where drug houses are, traffic patrolmen know where speeders are, and
custody officers learn where contraband is hidden within their facilities.
However, each assignment is different and requires a different type of
intelligence gathering.

What works in suburban areas will not work in inner-city locales.
What works in a lockup facility will not work in a maximum-security

prison. This requires intelligence gathering based upon our assignment. This is not profiling, which is contacting persons based upon race; it is old-fashioned police work.

Also, part of our training is to teach us to treat everyone respectfully. Nothing can get us into departmental hot water faster that to show disrespect or exhibit discrimination. Federal laws have been enacted to protect people who have been deprived of their civil rights or are victims of crimes committed by law enforcement under color of authority (18 U.S.C. §§ 241, 242). A separate police misconduct provision was added to cover state and local law enforcement (in addition to federal officers) from engaging in a pattern or practice of conduct that deprives persons of rights protected by the Constitution or laws of the United States (34 U.S.C. § 12601). Additionally, Title VI of the Civil Rights Act of 1964 and the Office of Justice Programs Statute also include the use of racial slurs as harassment as illegal.

These are just federal laws. Each state has their own laws, and I'm sure most counties and cities have ordinances that include areas of discrimination not covered by federal statute. It is never acceptable to withhold someone's civil liberties with malicious intent. However, it is often difficult to be proactive in seeking out and stopping crime with the threat of jail, lawsuit, or suspension hanging over our head. As usual, law enforcement is forced to walk a political tightrope. People want us to protect them, but at the expense of someone else. They want jails built to house criminals, but not in their neighborhood.

Christianity is much like this. God places us in certain situations based upon where we are at the time (our assignment). Through the Bible, we are trained to spread the Word (be proactive). We need to go to areas and meet with others so we can share Christ through our actions or what is written in the Bible (determine who the players are and where the crimes are committed). Intelligence gathering based upon the situation we have been placed in is also critical. What may work with our peers in the briefing room may not work at an after-shift meetup setting. What works with a victim of spousal abuse may not work with an inmate in custody.

We have been given a commandment by Christ to treat each other respectfully. The main difference between the human statues and Christ's commandment is love. We follow Christ's commandment out our love for him and the promise of life. We obey the human statute out of fear of punishment if we fail to comply.

> *So now I am giving you a new commandment: Love*
> *each other. Just as I have loved you, you should love*
> *each other. Your love for one another will prove to the*
> *world that you are my disciples.*
> —John 13:34–35

> *Jesus replied, "You must love the LORD your God*
> *with all your heart, all your soul, and all your mind.*
> *This is the first and greatest commandment. A second*
> *is equally important: 'Love your neighbor as yourself.'*
> *The entire law and all the demands of the prophets are*
> *based on these two commandments."*
> —Matthew 22:37–40

War Stories

Interacting with my dad's family was much different that my mom's family. My mom's family was nonjudgmental and accepting. My dad's family was not. At an early age, I learned certain words and witnessed certain attitudes that shocked me. African Americans, Hispanics, Asians, and Jews were all disparaged equally. My mom told me that when she met my dad's oldest brother for the first time, he told her that the family would love her whether she was a n———, Catholic, or a Jew. That pretty much sums up the sentiment of Dad's family.

When my dad's relative visited, my dad would always take me aside after the relative left the room and tell me what they had said was wrong.

He told me of incidents that he witnessed in Kentucky, of how African Americans were treated. It made him sick. As a man demonstrating the character of God, he would even correct his mother in front of all of us when she used such language.

My dad hosted a family reunion at our house in the mid-1960s. I sat with my parents, aunts, and uncles as they all discussed mixed-race marriages. I piped in that there was nothing wrong with this. My mom said this was how the young generation felt. As I was nine years old, I was then told to shut up. Looking at the event today, it could have been a Klan family barbecue.

I also remember answering a phone call in the mid-1960s. A man on the phone was spewing venom that African Americans and Jews were conspiring to take over America and that white America needed to stop this. I was about eight years old and gave the phone to my dad. My dad immediately hung up on the guy. I asked my parents about the call. They told me that the caller was a trying to drum up support to discriminate against African Americans and Jews and that he was a member of a group that only liked white people.

This treatment of nonwhites was not only limited to my dad's family. As I got older and would hang out at my friends' homes, their parents would make similar comments as my dad's family, only much milder.

My high school track coach, who was a member of a service club and a former drill instructor in the military, told me of an instance where a marine color guard was at a ceremony at his club. A few members of the color guard were African American.

I asked if the color guard stayed after the ceremony. He said no, but the white color guard members could have. I asked why the African Americans could not stay. He said, "That's just the way it is." I lost some respect for him that day.

If not for the strong influence and compassion demonstrated by my dad, I might have been indoctrinated into the sin of superiority and carried it into my career of law enforcement.

Government

Some of our views on discrimination have been instilled in us by our government. When we think of discrimination, we tend to think of Jim Crow in the South or the Separate but Equal doctrine of the federal government. I had a few friends raised in the South tell me of drinking from whites-only water fountains, and the beatings they took after getting caught by the police. My dad also told me of similar instances he witnessed as a kid in Kentucky.

Our country was based upon the freedom to worship God as we liked: Puritans in Massachusetts, Quakers in Pennsylvania, Catholics in Maryland, Anglicans in Virginia, Lutherans and Dutch Reformists in New York, and Baptists in the South. However, these colonists also brought scientific ideals from Europe learned via the Age of Enlightenment. Three of these ideals were: reconciling God and science, the opposition to religious philosophies, and scientific racism.

These three ideals were primarily of British origin and were upheld by several early Americans, including Thomas Jefferson, George Washington, and Thomas Paine. Jefferson went so far as to create his own Bible by cutting and pasting with a razor. This book discussed the moral lessons and teachings of Jesus, excluding the Resurrection and most examples of his divinity. The ideal of scientific racism held that whites are superior to other races, exemplified by both Jefferson and Washington owning slaves. As founders of the United States, their influence has been felt throughout our history—hence, the birth of white Anglo-Saxon Protestants.

Presidents

Teddy Roosevelt was an advocate of Eugenics. This was a "science" founded by Sir Francis Galton in the 1880s to biologically improve the human gene pool, using Anglo-Saxon, Nordic, and Germanic peoples as perfection. This science was the basis for genetic cleansing and the attempt to exterminate the Jews by the Nazis.

> *Society has no business to permit degenerates to re-*
> *produce their kind...Someday, we will realize that the*
> *prime duty, the inescapable duty, of the good citizen of*
> *the right type, is to leave his or her blood behind him in*
> *the world; and that we have no business to permit the*
> *perpetuation of citizens of the wrong type.*
> —Teddy Roosevelt

It should be noted among that Sir Francis Galton's other deeds was the belief that prayer was of no value based upon how long it took for prayers to be answered. For his services, he was knighted. He is also a half cousin of Charles Darwin—go figure that evil begets evil.

> *You can pray for anything, and if you have faith, you*
> *will receive it.*
> —Matthew 21:22

Woodrow Wilson signed legislation making interracial marriage illegal in Washington, DC. His reasoning was to "reduce the social friction building up in American society."

Hispanics and African Americans were segregated in the military under Wilson in World War I. When a delegation of African Americans went to the White House to protest, Wilson stated: "Segregation is not a humiliation but a benefit, and ought to be so regarded by you gentlemen."

> *Blacks can't run it. Nowhere, and they won't be able to*
> *for a hundred years, and maybe not for a thousand...Do*
> *you know maybe one black country that's well run?*
> —Woodrow Wilson

Franklin Roosevelt locked up over one hundred thousand Japanese Americans during World War ll and placed them in internment camps. German or Italian Americans were not singled out or treated in this manner.

Roosevelt invited all the athletes from the 1936 Olympic team to the White House—except the seventeen African Americans. This included Jesse Owens and Mack Robinson, older brother of Jackie Robinson. Jesse Owens stated, "Hitler didn't snub me—it was our president who snubbed me."

Richard Nixon said that he saw a future for the African American people, although he believed it would take five hundred years to accomplish: "They are coming along, and that after all they are going to strengthen our country in the end because they are strong physically and some of them are smart."

Of the six presidents listed above, five claimed to be Christian: Wilson and Teddy Roosevelt, Calvinist; George Washington and Franklin Roosevelt, Anglican; and Nixon, Quaker. Jefferson rejected Christianity. The five Christians did not act with compassion and mercy, as directed by our Savior. Jefferson is on his own. Their actions either created or furthered a divisiveness that continues today.

> *If anyone claims, "I am living in the light," but hates a*
> *fellow believer, that person is still living in darkness.*
> *Anyone who loves a fellow believer is living in the light*
> *and does not cause others to stumble. But anyone who*
> *hates a fellow believer is still living and walking in*
> *darkness. Such a person does not know the way to go,*
> *having been blinded by the darkness.*
> —1 John 2:9–11

Stand Tall

I by no means am advising to disregard our supervisors or leaders. We are directed to be subject to the governing authority.

> *Let everyone be subject to the governing authorities,*
> *for there is no authority except that which God has*

*established. The authorities that exist have been estab-
lished by God.*
—Romans 13:1

However, the Bible tells us to do be free of fear of authorities by doing what is right: "For rulers hold no terror for those who do right, but
for those who do wrong. Do you want to be free from fear of the one in
authority? Then do what is right and you will be commended" (Rom. 13:3).

*Remind the people to be subject to rulers and authori-
ties, to be obedient, to be ready to do whatever is good.*
—Titus 3:1

Following the hateful practices of our government listed above is not
right. For this reason alone, we must respectfully go against the directives in this area. There are many examples of the prophets and apostles
defying governmental edicts because they go against God. The greatest
act of defiance was at the Trial of Jesus. Jesus stated that he came to
overthrow the governments of this world because Satan had hardened
their hearts: "Don't imagine that I came to bring peace to the earth! I
came not to bring peace, but a sword. 'I have come to set a man against
his father, a daughter against her mother, and a daughter-in-law against
her mother-in-law. Your enemies will be right in your own household!'"
(Matt. 10:34–36).
Jesus was only given over to the Jews after appealing to Pilate's loyalty to the Roman government. In each of the four Gospels, Pilate only
cared about his own position and public loyalty to Caesar. He showed
no concern about the other accusations such as taxes, nor did Jesus deny
his Kingship, a seditious act. In other words, Pilate only cared about
self-survival: "Then Pilate tried to release him, but the Jewish leaders
shouted, 'If you release this man, you are no 'friend of Caesar.' Anyone
who declares himself a king is a rebel against Caesar'" (John 19:12).

History

When I was in a history class in college, I learned that California had the most antiminority laws than any other state in the country. Although California did not accept slavery upon statehood in 1850, California had laws against every other group.

Asians were brought to build railroads in California, but not allowed to buy property.

Native Americans were nearly wiped out, from approximately three hundred thousand in 1769 to seventeen thousand in 1900. This was started by the Spanish and continued by the federal government.

The first case to overturn school segregation occurred in California in 1947, *Mendez v. Westminster.* Several prestigious social and country clubs excluded Jews from memberships up until the 1980s.

California did not need to write laws to discriminate against African Americans; the Federal Housing Authority did it for them. From 1934 to 1968, the FHA would issue loans based on race. Nonwhites would be guided or "steered" to nonwhite areas to get a loan for a home. Also, "redlining" was used. This was the fencing off or "redlining" of an area, where the FHA would charge exorbitant rates to nonwhites.

Another act of legal racism in California occurred when Jackie Robinson was a kid living in Pasadena. African Americans were allowed to swim in the municipal pool, but only at the end of the month. The pool was drained, cleaned, and refilled immediately after use by African Americans.

In speaking with several retired officers from South Central Los Angeles before the 1965 Watts Riots, they told me of a radio call that referred to an African American in the city. Their description was not favorable. This was an accepted radio code. With this type behavior authorized by city fathers and used by officers, it is no wonder that prejudice was perpetuated by these departments. Only through the hiring of persons who truly represented the community was this behavior stopped.

I recently went to restaurant reopening, which was attended by the mayor, an African American woman. She stated that she was grateful to the original owner, who was in attendance and was about ninety-five years old, for serving her and her family as they drove to California from the South in the 1960s. I was appalled that "socially enlightened" California practiced this behavior in my lifetime.

How could Christians practice and enforce the sin of hate?

Anyone who hates another brother or sister is really a murderer at heart. And you know that murderers don't have eternal life within them. We know what real love is because Jesus gave up his life for us. So, we also ought to give up our lives for our brothers and sisters.

If someone has enough money to live well and sees a brother or sister in need but shows no compassion— how can God's love be in that person? Dear children, let's not merely say that we love each other; let us show the truth by our actions.
—1 John 3:15–18

For you are all children of God through faith in Christ Jesus. And all who have been united with Christ in baptism have put on Christ, like putting on new clothes. There is no longer Jew or Gentile, slave or free, male and female. For you are all one in Christ Jesus. And now that you belong to Christ, you are the true children of Abraham. You are his heirs, and God's promise to Abraham belongs to you.
—Galatians 3:26–27

War Stories

I was working swing shift in a primarily Hispanic station area. The field sergeant called for backup regarding a drunk driving traffic stop. Being a slow night, everyone responded. I got there and saw a well-dressed

African American man sitting on the curb. Being the youngest deputy at the time, I was going to volunteer to take the arrest.

I spoke to the man. He said that he was a musician and had just finished a gig at a local nightclub and was on his way home. I don't remember whether I saw any signs of intoxication.

I asked the sergeant why he stopped him. He said that he stopped him because he was black in the Hispanic station area. In my mind, my jaw hit the floor. I told him that it looked like there were enough deputies at the scene, so I left. I'm glad that I had not yet volunteered to take the handle on the call.

Another time, I was assigned to day shift, at the same station. I saw an African American man eating a breakfast in a park every weekday. We would wave at each other as I drove by. After about a week, I drove up to him to just talk. He worked at a defense contractor plant down the street.

We would talk about baseball or the Olympics. Always a short conversation, as I know what it is like to be disturbed while eating. I never asked him his name or for identification, as he was doing nothing wrong.

My captain called me into his office one day and said the city council had received reports of a black man in the park every morning. I knew what he was going ask me. Before he could finish, I told him that I'd spoken to him several times: "He works for a defense contractor. I did not get his name, nor will I, because he has done nothing wrong." My captain said, "Thank you, I'll let the city council know."

I'm ashamed to admit that I used racial slurs in the early part of my patrol career. Caucasians, African Americans, Asians, and Hispanics were all defamed. The words were used in describing individuals and not races. I did not and do not hate any person or race. The slurs were used very seldom and never to anyone's face. However, I still used these words and was wrong.

I don't buy into the argument that these were words used at the time. As I mentioned previously, my dad saw how African Americans were treated when he was a kid in the South. Yet I never heard him use any slanderous terms about any race. I should have known better.

Respect

> *You must be compassionate, just as your Father is compassionate. Do not judge others, and you will not be judged. Do not condemn others, or it will all come back against you. Forgive others, and you will be forgiven.*
> —Luke 6:36–37

In our line of work, we come across some of the most unusual and bizarre characters imaginable. Some of these folks look right out of a Hollywood movie. It is often difficult to deal with people whose lifestyles contradict ours. Although we may not understand or agree with some of the people we meet, everyone should receive the same protection and service. Remember, we are not to judge. The Lord does this.

War Stories

As a trainee, my training officer and I conducted a curfew patrol of a city park that closed at 10:00 p.m. It was about midnight. We saw a car with someone in the driver seat. We spoke with the driver, a man who had been drinking, and asked him to step out of the car to determine his level of intoxication. I asked for his license, which was in the glove box. He was very jittery as I opened the glove box. Inside the glove box was a woman's wig. When I asked him about the wig, he said that there were other wigs in the trunk and that we could search the car if we wanted. Of course, we searched the car.

As my training officer opened the trunk, he saw what at first looked like a woman's body. Upon further inspection, the contents turned out to be several other wigs rolled up in some women's dresses.

We checked to see if the man fit the suspect description of recent sex crimes in the area. He did not.

He said that he meets up with male friends at different locations for sex, and this night his meeting spot was the park. He was scared to death, as he told us that he was married with a couple of kids. He asked us not to tell his wife. We said that we don't judge, but he had to leave as the park closed at 2200 hours. As he was not intoxicated, he was allowed to leave. I learned from my training officer that night not to disrespect or verbally insult based upon a person's activity.

On another call, I responded to a call of a bar fight. The place ended up being a gay bar for Spanish-speaking patrons. Half of the men in the bar were in full drag; the other half were hitting on those in drag. Again, as the youngest deputy, I was assigned the handle. The veteran deputies were laughing at the patrons, calling them names in English and Spanish.

The fight was only a loud argument between two drunks over a drag queen with no punches thrown. I got the drunks to leave the bar without incident. One of the drag queens, who called himself Renee, became a good informant for me at that station. About a year after the bar incident, he gave me some information that led to the arrest of a gang member for murder.

As a sergeant, my watch commander sent me on a call of a white male in drag sitting in a recreational vehicle (RV) in the parking lot of an adult theater. The watch commander said that males exiting the theater would enter the RV and leave a few minutes later. I drove up and saw the RV and contacted the occupant. He was a thin white male with a ruddy complexion, about fifty-five to sixty, and in full drag. I sat down with the man at the table in the RV. I explained that he was in a gang-infested area where people may not understand his lifestyle.

I told him that it was not safe for him. I told him that I wasn't there to judge or belittle him; I just didn't want him to get hurt. He was very appreciative, telling me that I reminded him of his son, who was an officer in the military. He drove off shortly after I left.

Our attitudes of prejudice or superiority don't only include looking down at certain people because of the nine federally protected classes: sex, race, age, disability, color, creed, national origin, religion, or genetic information. The Bible tells us not to discriminate with persons of low position.

Live in harmony with one another. Do not be proud, but be willing to associate with people of low position. Do not be conceited.
—Romans 12:16

The Bible has numerous examples of discrimination and how Christ defeated this trial.

God used Cornelius, a man of faith, to show Peter that the Gentiles can be saved. Coupled with the vision of animals, it overcame Peter's prejudice toward the Gentiles: "Peter told them, 'You know it is against our laws for a Jewish man to enter a Gentile home like this or to associate with you. But God has shown me that I should no longer think of anyone as impure or unclean'" (Acts 10:28). Acts 10: 34–36 says, "Then Peter replied, "I see very clearly that God shows no favoritism. In every nation he accepts those who fear him and do what is right. This is the message of Good News for the people of Israel—that there is peace with God through Jesus Christ, who is Lord of all."

You may ask what did I do when I observed acts of bias or prejudice. A few times I brought up the issue to my supervisor. The supervisor was generally empathetic to the situation I discussed with him. Yet, with rare exception, there was nothing done.

If I saw a situation that particularly bothered me, I would speak with the deputy or peer. However, the most effective method that I used to correct prejudicial behavior was training, either as a training officer or through shift briefings that I conducted.

I was not afraid to discuss topics dealing with bias or prejudice with the troops. I did not use the phony departmental rhetoric. I spoke from experience, using some of the negative things that I had done as lessons learned. I told the troops that they may have personal sentiment that needs to be checked in the locker room. While they wore a uniform, they needed to be professional and fair—with a sense of humor.

Prejudice toward Law Enforcement

There was no law enforcement as we know today in biblical times, so Roman soldiers took the law enforcement role. Rome enforced its rule in the empire via its soldiers commanded by a centurion, and assisted by a tax collector. The tax collector was usually a Jewish man who went door to door to collect taxes for Rome. It was common knowledge that the collector would keep a portion of the taxes for themselves.

The disdain or persecution of law enforcement continues today. It is usually fueled from the corrupt actions of a small percentage of police officers, whether in the United States or in other countries. Having worked for the Los Angeles County Sheriff's Department (LASD) in multicultural Los Angeles County, I saw that the public's view of law enforcement could change from block to block. Some cultures view us as Roman soldiers in the Bible, and they taunted us verbally, while others were physically aggressive toward us.

Throughout the New Testament, there are several positive instances involving Roman soldiers and tax collectors. What makes this so remarkable is that Roman soldiers and tax collectors (law enforcement) were so despised by the Jews.

> *Even corrupt tax collectors came to be baptized and
> asked, "Teacher, what should we do?" He replied,
> "Collect no more taxes than the government requires."
> "What should we do?" asked some soldiers. John re-
> plied, "Don't extort money or make false accusations.
> And be content with your pay."*
> —Luke 3:12–14

Luke 7:6–10 tells the following story:

> So, Jesus went with them. But just before they arrived
> at the house, the officer sent some friends to say, "Lord,
> don't trouble yourself by coming to my home, for I am
> not worthy of such an honor. I am not even worthy to

come and meet you. Just say the word from where you are, and my servant will be healed."

I know this because I am under the authority of my superior officers, and I have authority over my soldiers. I only need to say, "Go," and they go, or "Come," and they come. And if I say to my slaves, "Do this," they do it.

When Jesus heard this, he was amazed. Turning to the crowd that was following him, he said, "I tell you; I haven't seen faith like this in all Israel!" And when the officer's friends returned to his house, they found the slave completely healed.

And this is found in Luke 19:2–10:

There was a man there named Zacchaeus. He was the chief tax collector in the region, and he had become very rich. He tried to get a look at Jesus, but he was too short to see over the crowd. So, he ran ahead and climbed a sycamore-fig tree beside the road, for Jesus was going to pass that way.

When Jesus came by, he looked up at Zacchaeus and called him by name. "Zacchaeus!'" he said. "'Quick, come down! I must be a guest in your home today." Zacchaeus quickly climbed down and took Jesus to his house in great excitement and joy. But the people were displeased. "He has gone to be the guest of a notorious sinner," they rumbled.

Meanwhile, Zacchaeus stood before the Lord and said, "I will give half my wealth to the poor, Lord, and if

I have cheated people on their taxes, I will give them
back four times as much!"

Jesus responded, "Salvation has come to this home
today, for this man has shown himself to be a true son
of Abraham. For the Son of Man came to seek and save
those who are lost."

Also, Matthew, one of the twelve apostles and author of one of the
Gospels, was a tax collector!

The Lord did not look down upon other despised classes of his day—
Samaritans and Gentiles. We need to follow his example and treat others
with the same mercy and compassion. Don't judge a book by its cover.
Remember, we all put our pants on the same way. No one is different.
We all have different cultures, ideas, and values. We need to look beyond
petty squabbles and work together, but not at the cost of our faith.

Satan

As usual, whatever the Lord does to show his glory, Satan copies to hide
the Lord's glory. As the Lord used biblical law enforcement in a positive way, Satan has used law enforcement in a negative way. Wikipedia
has created a list of incidents of civil unrest involving law enforcement
from 1960 to May 2020. There were eighty race riots on this list involving African Americans, Hispanics, and Puerto Ricans. Although I don't
have the documentation to make an educated determination as to who
was at fault in each situation, I am sure that police action either caused
or aggravated some of these situations. Remember that if Satan got to
Judas, he can surely get to us is if we don't have our Christian guard up
and wear the armor of God's righteousness.

As we know, law enforcement does the dirty work no one wants to
handle. People want to sit and point fingers and accuse us of police bru-
tality without offering viable solutions to racial situations. Although we
are in the executive branch of government and simply enforce the laws,

society has forced us to become experts in nearly social issue. The race related riots referred to above do not include riots associated with Vietnam, neo-Nazis, or political issues involving Antifa or other anarchist groups.

Sadly, we rarely get any support from the elected officials when a major riot or civil disturbance occurs. For the most part, these elected officials want to look like avengers for social justice. They are the ones who need to establish and maintain open channels of communication with all parties.

After a few concessions, these officials let the issue that created the riot die. In reality, nothing is accomplished. These officials just want to get reelected and dump off any further discussion to law enforcement. They are modern-day Pharisees.

Satan loves divisiveness. Only through our faith can we defeat Satan and the trial of prejudice.

> *Do not judge others, and you will not be judged. For you will be treated as you treat others. The standard you use in judging is the standard by which you will be judged.*
> —Matthew 7:1–2

> *Look beneath the surface so you can judge correctly.*
> —John 7:24

> *Instead, God chose things the world considers foolish in order to shame those who think they are wise. And he chose things that are powerless to shame those who are powerful. God chose things despised by the world, things counted as nothing at all, and used them to bring to nothing what the world considers important.*
> —1 Corinthians 1:27–28

Prejudice toward Each Other

*You have had enough in the past of the evil things that
godless people enjoy—their immorality and lust, their
feasting and drunkenness and wild parties, and their
terrible worship of idols.*

*Of course, your former friends are surprised when you
no longer plunge into the flood of wild and destructive
things they do. So, they slander you.*
—1 Peter 3:3–4

We also exhibit bias or prejudice among ourselves. In some stations where I've worked, officers are very cliquish and hang out together based upon race. This is bunk.

We depend on each other to go home after shift. Exhibiting racial attitudes, especially among ourselves, is not how Christ taught us and is a self-inflicted officer safety hazard. We all work for the same goal: keep our areas safe.

Some officers who do not discriminate and are equally compassionate to everyone are often chided or harassed. They are called "inmate lovers" in the jails. In patrol stations, the term is modified to reflect a racial slur.

Although the academy tried to teach empathy and cultural diversity, many officers either forgot these lessons or refused to release their preconceived ideas. We do not have the right to judge, especially if the person is a child of God.

Who are you to condemn someone else's servants?
Their own master will judge whether they stand or fall.
*And with the Lord's help, they will stand and receive his
approval.*
—Romans 14:4

*Here are some further sayings of the wise: It is wrong
to show favoritism when passing judgment. A judge who
says to the wicked, "You are innocent," will be cursed
by many people and denounced by the nations.*
—Proverbs 24:23–24

In addition to the bias exhibited by race, we also exclude others who do not fit with our lifestyle or off-duty activities. This often requires some type of initiation or "getting someone dirty" so the person can be trusted and accepted. The initiation could range from revelry to committing crimes. I've seen marriages broken up, alcoholics created, people being fired, and prison convictions handed down because of the want to be accepted. This is kind of like wanting to be one of the "cool kids" in high school. This could cause a brother or sister to fall.

War Stories

I asked a deputy whom I worked with why he got divorced. He said he wanted to be one of the boys and did what they did to be accepted. This included heavy drinking and carousing. He asked me how I stayed married while we worked together. I told him that I made promise to my wife and God that I would not cheat. I asked him if being one of the boys was why his marriage failed. He said yes. I told him that he was an idiot. Last I heard, he had gotten remarried and was happily married to her for over twenty years. I don't know if he is a believer, but it sounds to me like he learned to defeat the trial of infidelity.

Supervisors

As I've mentioned, most supervisors are good, if not outstanding. However, there are a few that fall well below this description. For some reason, you may have a supervisor who just doesn't like you and treats you unfairly. These types of supervisors are few and far between. But if you experience a bad one, this supervisor can tear you down—if you let him or her.

I had such a supervisor, who, along with his friends, blackballed me for over fifteen years.

War Stories

This sounds crazy, but this supervisor (captain) got angry with me for eating pasta with hot sauce instead of crushed red peppers. He was born in Italy and had become a US citizen at a very early age. When he saw me eating pasta with hot sauce, he said, "My mother would turn over in her grave if she saw you putting hot sauce on spaghetti!" He used a few other choice words as well. I told him that I did not have crushed peppers, only hot sauce. This was my first time that I had met the man.

A few months later, I was on the list to promote to sergeant. About three weeks before my promotion date, my captain opened IA investigations against me. My violation was looking at my brother's criminal record so I would not violate departmental procedure for associating with a felon.

Ordinarily, the detective sergeant would have handled this type of violation with a verbal admonishment or entry in the performance log; both were informal forms of discipline and removed after one year, having no impact on promotions. However, I was given formal discipline, which stayed permanently on my record and precluded any promotion until the discipline was completed.

My captain knew that I had to accept the formal discipline, or I could not be promoted. When I met with him to receive the discipline statement, he said, "You know, Blanks, just because you're leaving doesn't mean our paths won't cross again." I told him that I was never so happy to be disciplined, because now I could leave his command.

When I interviewed at three potential new assignments, I was turned down at each one. I found out later that the captains at each of these assignments were boating buddies of my captain. As a result, I received an assignment the farthest from my home—a jail facility eighty miles away. This was at the beginning of the 1992 Rodney King Riots, and when my former wife started stepping out on me.

After the riots stopped, the operations lieutenant at my new assignment asked me why I didn't try to get assigned to a unit closer to home. I told him I had gotten blackballed. He said that I was paranoid. A few days later after attending a custody division staff meeting, the lieutenant called me in his office and said, "Boy, you really pissed someone off! But I'm really glad to have you here." This meant a lot to me.

As my work location was very far from home, he said that I could put in for a hardship transfer to one of the units that had originally turned me down. I thanked the lieutenant but said I would rather stay where I was assigned. This was one of the best decisions I ever made. I really enjoyed my time at this facility. The people were great, and I got to teach patrol techniques to the deputies. I learned to how to quickly write administrative paperwork, as the riots were in full bloom. Also, I was given the collateral duty of a gang sergeant—a great job. Although my marriage went south, my walk with the Lord strengthened during the twenty-one months I was assigned at this facility. Through the Lord, I was able to clear my head through work.

A few years later, I was working at custody headquarters. A new division chief transferred in, one of the captains who had blackballed me when I tried to get assigned to his unit when I made sergeant. During his tenure, I took three lieutenant promotional exams. I never got promoted, although people with a lower score than me did.

During his tenure as chief, another friend of my former captain (who was now a commander), with whom I interviewed, became undersheriff. This was the number-two man in the department. Within a few weeks, this man told my chief that I had to be transferred from my custody headquarters job. He said that he had no confidence in my ability regarding statistics, although I had been commended by the Department of Justice and board of corrections for the accuracy of my reports. A commander, division chief, and the undersheriff—I guess when I make "special friends," I do it right.

The only position that I could find within the timeframe imposed by the undersheriff was at the courts—which was very slow, boring, and appealed to those in retirement mode. I made the best of what I considered a bad situation by asking the Lord for guidance and strength.

During my time in the courts, things were looking up. I met and married my wife. For some reason, the judge in charge of courthouse security of Los Angeles County starting relying on me for advice in courtroom safety matters, and I was given great autonomy by my supervisors. Also, my "special friends" who had blackballed me for over fifteen years had all retired. I was able to go back to my data and analysis job, where I worked with a great lieutenant and division chief who vocally supported me for promotion to lieutenant. I refused to let any of my "special friends" get to me. The Lord took care of me, gave me strength, and allowed me to get promoted to lieutenant in his time.

Trust not in human wisdom but in the power of God.
—1 Corinthians 2:5

It is better to take refuge in the Lord than to trust in princes.
—Psalms 118:8

Integrity

There will be no mercy for those who have not shown mercy to others. But if you have been merciful, God will be merciful when he judges you.
—James 2:13

Treat others the same way you want them to treat you.
—Luke 6:31

Guard your heart above all else, for it determines the course of your life. Avoid all perverse talk; stay away from corrupt speech. Look straight ahead, and fix your

*eyes on what lies before you. Mark out a straight path
for your feet; stay on the safe path. Don't get side-
tracked; keep your feet from following evil.*
—Proverbs 4:23–27

*Don't let anyone think less of you because you are
young. Be an example to all believers in what you say,
in the way you live, in your love, your faith, and your
purity.*
—1 Timothy 4:12

There have been numerous instances where I stopped a gang member or drug user for a minor crime. If the suspect was honest when I asked if the knife was his or when she used heroin last, they were released. This was respecting and rewarding the suspect's honesty. I actually learned how to correctly determine the age of injection marks from some addicts that I contacted. I also got many informants this way.

This goes for the jails as well. In my opinion, custody is a good place to break in your law enforcement career. Inmates are cooped up twenty-four seven and often want someone to talk to. Many times, if you speak with an inmate as you would anyone else, you get a positive response from him or her. They like to brag about their past crimes, just like they do to fellow inmates in the movies. They will often tell you how they broke into a house, how they stole a car, who is the "shot caller" or leader on the row, or who is moving drugs in a certain module or cellblock.

If you pay attention, you learn how to read people and tell if someone is being honest with you or lying. You come to realize that not everyone in jail is a bad guy. While some inmates made poor choices or dumb mistakes, they learn from their conviction, and you never see them again. Other inmates are in and out of jail so often that you remember them by name, and they remember you as well.

You learn that if you treat inmates in a firm and fair manner, you gain their respect through your integrity. Life for you and them is much easier. Often, this respect will follow you to the streets. On several occasions, inmates whom I worked with would come up and start talking to me. The first time this happened, I was on patrol training, and a guy walked up to me and yelled out my name—not called, but yelled. Turns out he was one of my inmate workers in the mess hall. He just wanted to chat. He was one of the shot callers of a local gang and became a good informant for me.

War Stories

My first assignment after graduating the academy was the Crip module. I had been assigned to this module for about two months. I was a baby-faced, blue-eyed, blond deputy who looked about fifteen years old, not twenty-three. The inmates were loud, violent Crip gang members from South Central Los Angeles, with many on parole. It doesn't get much more diversified that this. I was conducting the hourly safety check on the upper row while my partner was on another row—mistake number one was doing this when my partner was not watching. The row was about three feet wide and about fifteen feet aboveground.

As I opened the door to the fire escape to walk the row, I forgot that the cells were open and inmates were on free time—mistake number two. As I locked the fire escape door, I asked God to get me to through the row check safely. I was scared but could not show it. As I began my walk down the row, some of the inmates said, "Deputy, you ain't afraid to walk the row?" I answered, "No, I've never dissed you guys." They answered, "That's right." I finished walking the row, often having to sidestep the inmates to go around them.

I opened the door to the security booth, stepped in, and locked the door. I walked downstairs, out of inmate view, and took the deepest breath I had ever taken, and I thanked God that he had gotten me through this.

By following what I been taught by my Heavenly Father and reinforced by my earthly father—to treat others as you want to be treated—God protected me. When I told some of my peers what had happened, they were shocked that the inmates didn't rush to open the fire escape or injure me. I told them God must have felt that it was not my day to die. I still believe this.

What was the cost to treat an inmate like a human being? Time. I was there for at least eight hours. I would often give an inmate a cookie, extra food, or a cigarette. By doing this simple act, I was able to create a positive and respectful relationship with inmates. A few times when an inmate tried to attack me, another inmate would step in to back me up. Being firm, fair, respectful, and empathetic goes a long way.

However, you still need to wary and not let your guard down. This is gained only by training and experience.

> *A prudent person foresees danger and takes precautions. The simpleton goes blindly and suffers the consequences.*
> —Proverbs 22:3

War Stories

When I was a training officer, we arrested a child molester. My trainee wanted a piece of the suspect—very badly. I explained to him that any allegation of our misconduct could likely result in nonconviction in a jury trial. A defense attorney making an allegation of physical abuse or police misconduct only has to influence one jury member. The odds are pretty good that one jury member will fall prey to the defense attorney's accusation, whether the accusation is true or not.

My trainee was still hot after my explanation. I told him to sit in the car while I put cuffs on the suspect. I completely understood how my trainee felt, but he had to learn to control his emotions. That's what training is all about. Whether the training is from our department or from God, it is designed to improve our natural instincts, provide insight, and give wisdom—if we accept it. My trainee accepted the lesson and booked the suspect at the station in a calmer manner.

I loathe gangs, drugs, and crime—the activity, but not the person. I'm not so naive that I take a rose-colored view of people turning from criminal activity to God. Some people may come back to the Lord, but in reality, most won't. We generally only have a short timeframe when dealing with people in the streets, jails, or courts. Our actions are what people remember most. Our actions speak louder than words.

> *For we must all stand before Christ to be judged. We will each receive whatever we deserve for the good or evil we have done in this earthly body. Because we understand our fearful responsibility to the Lord, we work hard to persuade others. God knows we are sincere, and I hope you know this, too.*
> —2 Corinthians 5:10–11

Our profession and position on earth is temporary. Our position with Christ is permanent. Like the old Schlitz beer commercial said, "You only go around once in life." We do not get a second chance once we leave this planet. Don't give up what has been given to us.

> *For it is impossible to bring back to repentance those who were once enlightened—those who have experienced the good things of heaven and shared in the Holy Spirit, who have tasted the goodness of the word of God and the power of the age to come—and who then turn away from God. It is impossible to bring such people back to repentance; by rejecting the Son of God, they themselves are nailing him to the cross once again and holding him up to public shame.*
> —Hebrews 6:4–6

Bias against Other Christians

> *But you must not brag about being grafted in to replace the branches that were broken off. You are just a branch, not the root.*
> —Romans 11:18

Another form of bias is among Christians ourselves. This exclusion is not a major factor in our law enforcement life, but could be in our Christian life.

War Stories

As a sergeant, I was in a radio car with a deputy who yelled, "Pagans!" as we passed a group of people leaving a church service. Boy, did I rebuke him, not just from a departmental standpoint, but from a Christian perspective. He was a new Christian, and the group leaving the service were from a different Christian religion and held different beliefs than his. I reminded of the grafted olive branches.

> *"Well," you may say, "those branches were broken off to make room for me."*
>
> *Yes, but remember—those branches were broken off because they didn't believe in Christ, and you are there because you do believe. So, don't think highly of yourself, but fear what could happen. For if God did not spare the original branches, he won't spare you either.*
> *—Romans 11:19–22*

Paul wrote that we should accept believers who are weak. A believer is not just someone who follows what we believe, but what Jesus taught and who he is: "Accept other believers who are weak in faith, and don't argue with them about what they think is right or wrong" (Rom. 14:1).

> *Those who worship the Lord on a special day do it to honor him. Those who eat any kind of food do so to honor the Lord, since they give thanks to God before eating. And those who refuse to eat certain foods also want to please the Lord and give thanks to God. For we don't live for ourselves or die for ourselves. If we live,*

*it's to honor the Lord. And if we die, it's to honor the
Lord. So, whether we live or die, we belong to the Lord.*
—Romans 14:6–8

*So, because of your superior knowledge, a weak believ-
er for whom Christ died will be destroyed. And when
you sin against other believers by encouraging them to
do something, they believe is wrong, you are sinning
against Christ.*
—1 Corinthians 8:11–12

*For God so loved the world, that he gave his only be-
gotten Son, that whosoever believeth in him should not
perish, but have everlasting life. For God sent not his
Son into the world to condemn the world; but that the
world through him might be saved. He that believeth
on him is not condemned: but he that believeth not is
condemned already, because he hath not believed in the
name of the only begotten Son of God.*
—John 3:16–18 (KJV)

I used the King James Version instead of the New Living Translation
for John 3:16–18. The New Living Translation does not incorporate the
word "begotten" in these verses. I believe that *begotten* is too important
to be left out. The term *begotten* shows that Jesus is, of, and equal to God
the Father. This is why the Pharisees and leaders of the law persecuted
him. If Jesus claimed to be only a created man or messenger of God, like
Abraham, Moses, or John, then prophecy would not have been fulfilled.

When Jesus claimed that he was "I am," the leaders of the law knew
that he was claiming to be God and not a man or created being. Jesus
was stating that he is eternal, with no beginning and no end—only God
is eternal with no beginning and no end. While on this planet, Jesus was
a man with limited time on earth. In reality, he is eternal, not created,
with no beginning and no end. He has always been with the Father and

the Holy Spirit. The three are distinct persons that make up God and are documented in the verses below.

The Father acknowledges that Jesus is God:

> But to the Son he says, "Your throne, O God, endures forever and ever. You rule with a scepter of justice. You love justice and hate evil. Therefore, O God, your God has anointed you, pouring out the oil of joy on you more than on anyone else." (Heb. 1:8)

> He also says to the Son, "In the beginning, Lord, you laid the foundation of the earth and made the heavens with your hands." (Heb. 1:10)

> And God never said to any of the angels, "Sit in the place of honor at my right hand until I humble your enemies, making them a footstool under your feet." (Heb. 1:13)

> Thus, the heavens and the earth, and all the host of them, were finished. (Gen. 2:1, KJV; *again, I used the King James Version to show that angels were created, not eternal like God.*)

The Father states that Jesus created the heavens and earth and was witnessed by the Holy Spirit:

> And now in these final days, he has spoken to us through his Son. God promised everything to the Son as an inheritance, and through the Son he created the universe. (Heb. 1:1)

> In the beginning God created the heavens and the earth. The earth was formless and empty, and darkness

covered the deep waters. And the Spirit of God was hovering over the surface of the waters. (Gen. 1:1–2)

Stay True to the Word

Although there are several issues influencing our biases and prejudices, we can defeat them all by remaining true to our faith as Christians. We need to stick to what the Bible says, not man-made theory or dogmas as to what we think God wants. We can't pick and choose what to follow. We must follow what we were taught and fight the good fight. We may stumble on our walk, but if we truly believe, we will not fall. We will have God to support us, whether in the person of the Father, Son, or Holy Spirit.

Don't be afraid, for I am with you. Don't be discouraged, for I am your God. I will strengthen you and help you. I will hold you up with my victorious right hand.
—Isaiah 41:10

Teach these new disciples to obey all the commands I have given you. And be sure of this: I am with you always, even to the end of the age.
—Matthew 28:20

And I will ask the Father, and he will give you another Advocate, who will never leave you. He is the Holy Spirit, who leads into all truth.
—John 14:16–17

CHAPTER 3

Taming the Tongue

Indeed, we all make many mistakes. For if we could control our tongues, we would be perfect and could also control ourselves in every other way. We can make a large horse go wherever we want by means of a small bit in its mouth. And a small rudder makes a huge ship turn wherever the pilot chooses to go, even though the winds are strong.

In the same way, the tongue is a small thing that makes grand speeches. But a tiny spark can set a great forest on fire. And among all the parts of the body, the tongue is a flame of fire. It is a whole world of wickedness, corrupting your entire body. It can set your whole life on fire, for it is set on fire by hell itself.

People can tame all kinds of animals, birds, reptiles, and fish, but no one can tame the tongue. It is restless and evil, full of deadly poison. Sometimes it praises our Lord and Father, and sometimes it curses those who have been made in the image of God. And so, blessing and cursing come pouring out of the same mouth. Surely, my brothers and sisters, this is not right!

> *Does a spring of water bubble out with both fresh water
> and bitter water? Does a fig tree produce olives, or a
> grapevine produce figs? No, and you can't draw fresh
> water from a salty spring.*
> —James 3:1–12

This kind of reminds me of a scene in the movie, *Wayne's World*, in which Garth is chewing out Wayne, with numerous swear words. Wayne responds, "Kiss your mother with that mouth?"

Once something is said, it is impossible to retract it.

> *Death and life are in the power of the tongue, and those
> who love it will eat its fruits.*
> —Proverbs 18:21

> *A good man brings good things out of the good stored
> up in his heart, and an evil man brings evil things out
> of the evil stored up in his heart. For the mouth speaks
> what the heart is full of.*
> —Luke 6:45

> *Let no corrupting talk come out of your mouths, but
> only such as is good for building up, as fits the occa-
> sion, that it may give grace to those who hear.*
> —Ephesians 4:29

> *It is not what goes into the mouth that defiles a person,
> but what comes out of the mouth; this defiles a person.*
> —Matthew 15:11

The main theme is the power of words, as they speak of what is on our hearts. When we are cursed and abused, it is usually during an emotionally charged call for service such as domestic abuse, mental health, drugs/alcohol, teen rebellion, or just plain hate of law enforcement. In most cases we have done nothing to the person, and we are persecuted simply because we wear a uniform and represent authority.

Responding in kind to the garbage being spewed does nothing but make the situation worse. Believe me, I would have loved to have given a sarcastic response to verbal junk being thrown at me, but I learned that it does no good.

> *If a wise man has an argument with a fool, the fool only rages and laughs, and there is no quiet.*
>
> *Those who worship the Lord on a special day do it to honor him. Those who eat any kind of food do so to honor the Lord, since they give thanks to God before eating. And those who refuse to eat certain foods also want to please the Lord and give thanks to God. For we don't live for ourselves or die for ourselves. If we live, it's to honor the Lord. And if we die, it's to honor the Lord. So, whether we live or die, we belong to the Lord.*
>
> *Again, I say, don't get involved in foolish, ignorant arguments that only start fights. A servant of the Lord must not quarrel but must be kind to everyone, be able to teach, and be patient with difficult people.*
> —2 Timothy 2:23–24

Taming the tongue not only refers to words, but also our actions. What is on our hearts cannot only be heard, but seen and felt as well. A musician can let us know what they are feeling as their emotions flow from their hands. People also use their hands to show anger and other negative emotions via physical gestures.

If we let sinful emotions such as anger, hate, and jealousy rule us, then these sins will be responsible for what comes from our heart. Our words and actions are controlled by our human nature. We can't help it—but with God, we can.

> *For this very reason, make every effort to add to your
> faith goodness; and to goodness, knowledge; and to
> knowledge, self-control; and to self-control, persever-
> ance; and to perseverance, godliness; and to godliness,
> mutual affection; and to mutual affection, love. For if
> you possess these qualities in increasing measure, they
> will keep you from being ineffective and unproductive
> in your knowledge of our Lord Jesus Christ.*
> —2 Peter 1:5–8

Good or Evil

Words and actions can be used for either good or evil purposes. The greatest act of good is the death of Jesus. His words were powerful, but his actions were stronger. God made a promise to us and kept his word through the most painful way possible: the death of his only Son for a generation of ungrateful sinners. Thank you, Lord!

The greatest act of evil was Satan deceiving Eve in the Garden of Eden. Through his actions, Satan duped Eve into believing that he was wiser than God. He misinformed her that she would be equal with God if she ate the fruit from the Tree of Knowledge. She and Adam failed in their first test of following God's word. This was the first example of Satan deceiving us by twisting God's words. There are many other acts of this in the Bible. I listed these two as examples.

In Genesis 4, Cain, jealous of his brother Abel, made a plan to murder his brother. Cain summoned Abel to meet with him. Cain, lying in wait, jumped on his brother and stuck a knife in his back, killing Abel. Cain consciously devised a (premeditated) plan and carried it through, committing the first murder described in the Bible.

Acts 5 tells of Ananias, who lied about the price of a property that he sold. He donated the proceeds, giving the money to Peter, who knew that Ananias lied about the amount the property sold for. When Peter asked if the money donated was the amount of the sale, Ananias said yes. Peter rebuked him for lying to God. Ananias instantly fell dead. A few hours later, Ananias's wife walked in and lied to Peter about the proceeds of the property. She, too, fell dead instantly.

Revelation states that many will voluntarily have the mark of the beast placed upon them, as part of Satan's premeditated plan to attempt to defeat God. People will worship evil (the beast) based upon Satan's scheme to make our own desires our priority and not the desires of God. Although we don't know what the mark will be, we don't need to worry. Through grace and truly following Christ, we will be saved, and our names will be written in the Book of Life. Perseverance and wisdom gained through Jesus will show us how to stay aligned with the Lord, and not succumb to Satan's plan.

Training

In law enforcement, there are times when we must act immediately. These are the instances for which we train so that our training replaces our natural response with a correct response. Following Christ also replaces our human response with a perfect God-inspired response. We don't always follow God's perfect response. If we did, then we would not need any additional training. Even Paul acknowledges his need for training: "All athletes are disciplined in their training. They do it to win a prize that will fade away, but we do it for an eternal prize. So, I run with purpose in every step. I am not just shadowboxing. I discipline my body like an athlete, training it to do what it should" (1 Cor. 9:25–27).

Two biblical examples of handling critical or impromptu situations involve Joseph and Jesus. Joseph's brothers sold him into slavery and then lied to Jacob for years that Joseph was killed by wild animals. Joseph reacted by trusting (training) in God, who made Joseph second in command of all Egypt through Pharaoh. He saved Jacob and his brothers—Israel and the twelve tribes.

During the Trial of Jesus, the Sanhedrin stirred up the crowds into demanding that Jesus be crucified. When Pilate was accused of treason against Caesar, he turned Jesus over to be crucified. Jesus had prepared (trained) for this moment for years. The result was Jesus dying on a cross for all of our sins.

The Sanhedrin acted as other anarchists have throughout history, stirring up people for unlawful or immoral acts by chaos. Although the Sanhedrin had planned for years to kill Jesus, the words and actions of the crowd were unplanned and instantaneous. We have seen many acts of anarchy today and within the last one hundred years: fascism, Nazism, Communism, student riots, Islamic terrorists, and Antifa.

However, in most instances, we don't need to act hastily or impulsively. After we have quelled the immediate threat, we have the luxury of time. This does not mean we can waste hours handling a nonemergent call; it means we have time to formulate a plan or conduct an investigation. We are afforded the opportunity to put our training into practice into use and fully utilize what we have been taught. It also gives us time to tame our tongues and control our actions.

> *An angry person starts fights; a hot-tempered person commits all kinds of sin.*
> —Proverbs 29:22

> *A hot-tempered person starts fights; a cool-tempered person stops them.*
> —Proverbs 15:18

I mentioned that we usually have time on our side to control our emotions. However, there are times when we have less than split second to control our emotions.

You are driving in a perilous vehicle pursuit, get the car stopped with guns drawn, and then place handcuffs on the suspect.

You and your partner get into a fight with a suspect.

A riot breaks out in jail module, and inmates try to injure you or your partners while you are dispersing the event.

These are difficult issues to deal with. We support each other and don't let suspects put their hands on us. There are times when we must use force in making an arrest, sometimes resulting in the suspect becoming injured. I've sent a few suspects to the hospital when my peers or myself were threatened physically. It was justified. There were also a few times when force to injure a suspect was justified per policy, but I did not feel right in using that amount of force. In these instances, my watch commander would ask me why the suspect wasn't booked at the hospital. I told him that amount of force was not necessary.

> *Don't sin by letting anger control you. Don't let the sun*
> *go down while you are still angry, for anger gives a*
> *foothold to the devil.*
> —Ephesians 4:26–27

We get paid to do a job that no one wants to do. This includes having to turn off our emotions like a light switch and treating the suspect respectfully. Peter had an issue with controlling himself immediately following an emotional event.

In Luke 22:49–51, Peter cuts off the ear of Malchus, servant of the high priest Caiaphas, at the arrest of Jesus. Having been involved in many force incidents both as a deputy and as a supervisor, I'm sure that Peter was not aiming at Malchus's ear or Malchus at all. He most likely was going after Judas or Caiaphas. Much like a supervisor, Jesus stopped the assault and rebuked Peter. Unlike a supervisor, Jesus replaced the ear.

War Stories

I chased a guy in a vehicle pursuit for driving under the influence. The guy pulled into his driveway and ran into his house before I could catch him. As I was still in fresh pursuit, I put out a broadcast and continued to watch the house until backup arrived. The smell of PCP reeked from inside the suspect's car. Once the troops were set, I knocked on the door. The guy opened the screen door in front. I lunged through the screen door, knocking my sergeant on his keister. I placed cuffs on and arrested the suspect without incident. I was a bit excited but knew better than to thump the suspect once he was in custody. My sergeant chuckled, telling me later that he didn't expect me run through the screen door, thus knocking him on his rear end. My sergeant was Malchus in this instance. He got between me and the suspect, who was definitely going to jail.

I was a sergeant at our largest jail facility, housing nearly ten thousand male inmates at the time. A large fight broke out in one of the gang rows, so I responded to monitor the deputies. I saw one of my deputies kick a handcuffed inmate lying on his side in the rear one time. When the incident was over, I took him aside and spoke to him. The deputy was very new and excited. He was also a good worker and had not demonstrated this type of behavior previously.

He told me that he shouldn't have kicked the inmate and was very contrite. I explained to him that the next time that I witnessed this, I would have to document the event. I basically gave him a good old-fashioned country rear-end chewing, as the force was out of policy but not egregious. Much like a parent, I reinforced his good qualities but did not condone his actions.

Tit for Tat

In our world, we deal with people who are at their worst or can't stand authority. When verbally challenged, our natural inclination is to go "eye for an eye" or "tit for tat." As difficult as it sounds (and it is), we are trained to look beyond these verbal barbs. Notice that I said *verbal barbs*, not *physical attacks*.

I've been called every name in the book, both in English and Spanish. I've been called a flesh-eating blue-eyed devil, gestapo, and pig and other names that I won't write down. As I mentioned earlier in this book, I did not always respond as Christ directed me to. However, his training via the Holy Spirit gave me ability to let these verbal barbs fly off.

> *A truly wise person uses few words; a person with*
> *understanding is even-tempered. Even fools are thought*

*wise when they keep silent; with their mouths shut, they
seem intelligent.*
—Proverbs 17:27–28

I've seen many instances of law enforcement officers responding "tit for tat" in response to verbal barbs. Sometimes the officer had a bad day and sometimes it was just the officer's way of handling a situation. We were trained to respond to a situation in the manner that the person would understand. This meant that we would deal with situations on their level so a situation could be handled professionally, respectfully, and positively. Some officers interpreted this as responding in kind to how we were treated. This was not the message. We were not taught to talk down or insult someone.

War Stories

When I was a young deputy, an eighteen- or nineteen-year-old college student yelled, *"Pig!"* as I drove by. I got mad. I stopped and got in the kid's face. He started crying and apologized out of fear, not remorse. My intent was to get back at him for disrespecting me. I should have handled this differently. He posed no threat to me.

A few years later, I was working in South Central Los Angeles during the time that Crips and Bloods were at their heyday. When I would stop a gang member, they would suck their teeth. This was telling me to have sex with myself. Many deputies took this as a personal insult. I didn't. I laughed at them and told them that they were silly. Some of them were shocked that I did not get angry, and they would stop acting up. Others tried harder to upset me. Still, I didn't bite. Since their actions were not physical, why give them the satisfaction of getting what they wanted, which was to upset me? There were others whose actions were physical. They were handled differently.

As a one-man car in South Central Los Angeles, I arrested a man for selling drugs. He was about 6'3" and well over 400 pounds. I'm 5'11 on a good day and weighed about 185 pounds. The man told me that I was taking food out of his family's mouth because of the arrest. He said that he wouldn't let himself be arrested—although in a bit stronger language. I immediately asked the Lord for help.

I told him that I would call for additional deputies and that both of us would get hurt, but he was going to jail. I told him that I would let him finish eating his lunch and then the cuffs would go on. He agreed. I'm glad I carried extra cuffs, as it took three cuffs to get his arms behind his back. This plan was definitely not my own; thank you, Jesus! I did not plan to arrest the man on that day. It was an instantaneous event, and I relied on my training to handle the arrest successfully.

Anger

> *If you claim to be religious but don't control your tongue, you are fooling yourself, and your religion is worthless. Pure and genuine religion in the sight of God the Father means caring for orphans and widows in their distress and refusing to let the world corrupt you.*
> —James 1:25–27

Often our emotions (tongues) rule our decision-making. When people refuse to comply with our lawful directives, we often get angry. We tend to refer to that person in a less-than-positive light or with a description that defames them. I have.

War Stories

I worked undercover in high school when I first came on the sheriff's department. After the program ended, we had a party at the supervising lieutenant's home. I remember the supervising sergeant telling me how to work patrol. He said he would always ticket someone who passed his radio car as "contempt of cop." As he told me this story, he slandered the person with an insulting description and became angry. The sergeant took this as a personal insult. I was very young and impressionable, but I knew this was wrong. Getting angry because someone passed you while that person was doing the speed limit? Wow, what a message to send to a kid with thirty years of service ahead of him!

Remember that we usually see people at their worst when we contact them. If they have authority issues when they are calm, imagine what they will be like when emotionally charged. Usually, the instances where we give a directive is not an emergent situation, and we have time to regroup or collect our thoughts. We can either explain the reason for the directive or explain what will happen if they continue in noncompliance to the request. This is where our training comes in, from both our department and the Bible. If we have not adhered to our training, becoming second nature, anger wells up in us. This anger can cause us abuse others either verbally or physically.

War Stories

I have a brother who was arrested for a narcotics charge while he was still living with my parents in the mid-1980s. The local police conducted a search warrant of my parents' home, recovering several pieces of evidence. Right after the warrant was completed, my mom called my station, leaving a message with the watch sergeant.

When I called her back, she was livid. She said that she followed the police around the house and became upset when they took several items belonging to my brother. She is definitely not the most receptive person when given a directive. She said that they threatened her with arrest if she did not sit down. She used a few words that I had never heard her use before in describing the police and the incident. Obviously, she was not at her best that evening.

I asked my dad what happened during the warrant service. He told me that the police were very curt when entering the house but relaxed after they made entry. They were not disrespectful and spent some time trying to explain the situation to my mom. I felt compassion for the officers serving the warrant. I love my mom, but I told her that she had to do what she told. Our relationship has never been the same since this time. Although she has mellowed a bit, she still has a disdain for law enforcement.

We sometimes get angry when a suspect is released before the end of shift or the district attorney refuses to file one of our arrests. We sometimes forget that as law enforcement officers, we arrest and detain suspects. The duty of doling out punishment is for judges, based upon what the legislature has decided. It is not our duty to mete out justice or punishment. This is known as "curbside justice." I've witnessed this more often in jails than on the streets. Don't get me wrong: I believe that persons should be held accountable for their actions. There have been times, both in the jails and in the streets, when an individual took up a combative stance, posing a threat to either my safety or that of someone else. They were handled appropriately. Sometimes they were injured, other times not. However, we aren't the ones to mete out justice or sentences.

We know most suspects will not be convicted or sentenced correctly for their crimes. I'll cite a few California laws that show how this has negatively impacted public safety.

In November 2014, California voters passed Proposition 47, which removed wobbler felony arrests. A wobbler felony is a crime that a charged as either a felony or misdemeanor. For example, if someone was arrested for petty theft with a prior conviction or possession of heroin, the person would have been charged with a felony and held for forty-eight hours. This gave detectives time to investigate. Now, these persons are arrested for a misdemeanor, and in most cases released on a citation before the end of the arresting officer's shift.

Another law voted in was Proposition 57 in November 2016. This law allowed for the early release of nonviolent criminals from prisons. Proposition 57 allows repeat offender inmates with multiple offenses, the same release parameters as first-time single-offense offenders. In most cases, prior violent offenses are not included in determining nonviolent releases.

A third law is the Public Safety Realignment Act of 2011, which was eventually implemented as part of Assembly Bill 109 in 2018. This removed nonviolent parolees from state jurisdiction and placed them on county probation departments as probationers. This was not done for humanitarian reasons; it was done as a cost savings method for the state of California, not for local counties and cities.

The results of criminal reform were a 25 percent increase in homelessness, a 13 percent increase in violent crime, and a 46 percent increase in rape since the implementation of these laws. Additionally, there were 330,000 inmates freed on early release during the same four-year period. The number of early release inmates is roughly the same as the entire population of St. Louis, Pittsburgh, or Cincinnati. The results of these laws are frustrating, to say the least. This often leads to administrating curbside justice or severe apathy—either one removes our ability to act as professional law enforcement officials.

War Stories

A deputy was providing security in the hallway during morning chow. I was the mess hall officer. We fed two thousand inmates in about ninety minutes. There would be up to two hundred inmates lined up on both sides of the hallway at any given time during chow. There were maybe three deputies in the hallway.

An inmate with some type of mental issue yelled something at the deputy, who got angry and smacked the inmate across the back with his flashlight. This caused a commotion among the inmates in the hallway. One of the other deputies in the hallway grabbed the deputy with the flashlight and sent him into the control booth. Another deputy took the inmate and placed him in a room with a window, and he was dealt with after chow, which was procedure. The actions of these two deputies calmed the nearly two hundred inmates in the hallway. The inmates knew that these two deputies had acted correctly regarding the actions of inmate with mental issues. The deputy with the flashlight became angry. He felt that he was disrespected and had doled out "curbside justice."

Another time, I had a training officer in the jails call me into the shower room after morning chow. He had brought an inmate with him and told me to punch the inmate because he continually stole food from the chow line, causing disruptions. He referred to the inmate in a less-than-stellar manner. I told him no.

This inmate had some minor mental issues and posed no threat to me nor anyone else. The inmate took an extra apple or hard-boiled egg—big deal. At most, the inmate should have been reprimanded per jail rules. I was shocked at the request and walked away. My training officer thought he had the right to dispense punishment because the inmate violated some minor jail rules. This made the deputy angry. Needless to say, on paper, I never got off training.

There was a particular inmate who had a court order for extra milk and cottage cheese because of ulcers. The crimes for which he was convicted were particularly gruesome, with the victims all being very young prostitutes. This inmate received his court-ordered milk and cottage cheese. There was a large ladle of grease placed on the bottom of the cottage cheese, and his milk was expired. The court order read "milk and cottage cheese." It did not say what condition the dairy items were to be in. I did this out my sentiment for the victims he had killed. My Superman cape and big *S* on my chest came out. There were cop killers, prison gang leaders, and other violent career criminals in this module, but I was able to act professionally and impartially in my dealings with these inmates. The crimes committed by this particular inmate got to me. In a way, I was playing judge, and that was wrong.

I was assigned a domestic violence call. Then informant was anonymous. This occurred when domestic violence was yet not considered a crime. The couple was about the same age as I was. He was drunk, belligerent, and antagonistic. She was scared to death. As there were no laws to arrest him, I shoved him against the wall and told him that if another call came from that residence, I would personally kick his ass and take him to jail. I have an issue with spousal abuse, whether the man or woman is the victim. Again, the *S* on my chest popped out, and I felt the need to protect his wife. We never did receive another call. However, I was wrong.

My partner and I had a juvenile disturbance call. Two sixteen-year-old boys in a condo complex had verbally harassed the wife of one of the residents. We separated the boys and asked them what happened. I told the kid that I was talking to that he was lucky the husband did not thump him. The kid made some type of insulting remark about the couple and then about me and my partner. I smacked the kid on the side of his face. He had made me angry.

My partner looked at me with surprise, as this was out of character for me. We took the kid home and were met by his father and his father's boyfriend, who was the dominant one in the relationship. After a few minutes, we left. I apologized to the kid. I understood why he acted out. However, his home life didn't give him the right to act as he did. Nor did I have the right to act as I did.

As you can see, I've have fallen prey to anger too. I have learned from my actions, reminding myself not to let personal sentiment cloud my actions in the future. I still had situations where my emotions got the best of me, but I was generally able to distance myself from acting as normal person instead of a Christian law enforcement officer. I remember what a judge once said during a sentencing hearing: "I must divorce myself from sentiment, and sentence as prescribed by law." We have to remember that we enforce the law, not judge, and we do not mete out punishment. We cannot allow our emotions to make us the avenger or to wear the big *S* on our chests.

Dear friends, never take revenge. Leave that to the righteous anger of God. For the Scriptures say, "I will take revenge; I will pay them back," says the Lord. Do all that you can to live in peace with everyone. Never pay back evil with more evil. Do things in such a way that everyone can see you are honorable.
—Romans 12:17–19

Understand this, my dear brothers and sisters: You must all be quick to listen, slow to speak, and slow to get angry. Human anger does not produce the righteousness God desires. So, get rid of all the filth and evil in your

*lives, and humbly accept the word God has planted in
your hearts, for it has the power to save your souls.
But don't just listen to God's word. You must do what it
says. Otherwise, you are only fooling yourselves.*
—James 1:19–20

Righteous Indignation or Anger

In writing this book, I came upon the term "righteous indignation." This is anger caused by passion to overcome sin and what God considers injustice. Several times throughout the Bible, we see God the Father; his Son, Jesus; prophets; and apostles get angry. However, in these instances, the anger was over the failure to worship or give glory to God.

God himself became angry. In 2 Samuel 12, God's anger was relayed to David by Nathan after David murdered Uriah in order to marry his wife, Bathsheba. Although David repented of his sin, David was punished. His son with Bathsheba died after seven days. However, God showed mercy to David and gave him another son, Solomon.

God is an honest judge. He is angry with the wicked every day. If a person does not repent, God will sharpen his sword; he will bend and string his bow. He will prepare his deadly weapons and shoot his flaming arrows.
—Psalms 7:11–13

They will never even see the land I swore to give their ancestors. None of those who have treated me with contempt will ever see it.
—Numbers 14:23

So, he stood at the entrance to the camp and shouted, "All of you who are on the Lord 's side, come here and join me." And all the Levites gathered around him.

Moses told them, "This is what the Lord, the God of Israel, says: Each of you, take your swords and go back and forth from one end of the camp to the other. Kill everyone—even your brothers, friends, and neighbors." The Levites obeyed Moses' command, and about 3,000 people died that day.

Then Moses told the Levites, "Today you have ordained yourselves for the service of the Lord, for you obeyed him even though it meant killing your own sons and brothers. Today you have earned a blessing."
—Exodus 32:26–30

In Matthew 23, Jesus becomes angry at the Pharisees and teachers of the law for shutting the door to the kingdom of heaven to those who follow the law and disregard God. Jesus refers to Jewish leaders as "blind guides," "vipers," "snakes," and "hypocrites." I would say Jesus was passionately angry over what the Pharisees were teaching and the injustice rendered by them upon the Jews.

He looked around at them angrily and was deeply saddened by their hard hearts. Then he said to the man, "Hold out your hand." So, the man held out his hand, and it was restored!
—Mark 3:5

Jesus made a whip from some ropes and chased them all out of the Temple. He drove out the sheep and cattle, scattered the money changers' coins over the floor, and turned over their tables. Then, going over to the people who sold doves, he told them, "Get these things out of here. Stop turning my Father's house into a marketplace!" Then his disciples remembered this prophecy

*from the Scriptures: "Passion for God's house will
consume me."*
—John 2:15–17

John the Baptist and Paul also exhibited righteous indignation when it came to the Gospel: "But when he saw many Pharisees and Sadducees coming to watch him baptize, he denounced them. 'You brood of snakes!' he exclaimed. 'Who warned you to flee God's coming wrath? Prove by the way you live that you have repented of your sins and turned to God'" (Matt. 3:7–8).

*But when Peter came to Antioch, I had to oppose him to
his face, for what he did was very wrong. When he first
arrived, he ate with the Gentile believers, who were
not circumcised. But afterward, when some friends of
James came, Peter wouldn't eat with the Gentiles any-
more. He was afraid of criticism from these people who
insisted on the necessity of circumcision. As a result,
other Jewish believers followed Peter's hypocrisy, and
even Barnabas was led astray by their hypocrisy.*
—Galatians 2:11–13

There have been a few instances in my career where I was angry based upon injustice.

War Stories

After inmate chow, there was always a lot of food that got thrown out. I asked my sergeant if we could give the food to homeless shelters in downtown Los Angeles. He agreed and brought the issue to the captain. The captain agreed and brought the issue to county counsel, who shot the idea down. County counsel was afraid of lawsuits if anyone became sick from eating the food. I used to eat inmate or main line chow. It was safe; inmates are not going mess with their own food.

I offered to write a document that would waive a person's right to sue after eating jail food. County counsel again refused. I told them that it was a sin to waste the food. They didn't care. I brought this issue up each time I was assigned to custody, four times over my thirty-two-year career. Each time, county counsel refused.

I was on patrol training on my first day with my new training officer. We received a child welfare call. There was a mother and four children, ages four to sixteen, living in a converted chicken coop. The coop had a door, was clean, and contained beds. There was a stove and refrigerator, plenty of food, and the children were all happy and immaculate. Their clothes reminded me of the verse from the Stevie Wonder song "Living for the City": "Her clothes are old, but never are they dirty."

However, there were no sanitation facilities, and the electricity came from an extension cord from the house. We had to remove the children upon the directive of the Department of Children and Family Services. The mother spoke Spanish only, so I had to tell her that we were removing her children.

As you can imagine, she cried and screamed violently, tearing her clothes in deep mental anguish. She had done nothing wrong except to want a better life for her kids. I was probably the angriest that I had ever been in my career. I wanted to arrest the landlord in the house, who was the informant. He had called because the woman was behind in her rent. Per the law, there was nothing I could do to the landlord.

As my training officer and I pulled into the station at the end of shift, I told him I wanted to go to a law library and dig up some sections to use against the landlord. He said that the matter of rent was a civil issue and the immigration issue a federal matter. He said, "I understand. Don't ever lose your passion." When it came to mothers and children, I never did.

Another time, I was getting my report read in the field just before the end of shift—yes, at a doughnut shop. I saw a thirteen- or fourteen-year-old kid slap his mother in the face. I got out of the car, grabbed the kid under the armpit, and began to speak to his mother. My sergeant said, "Bob, let go." After a few seconds, he said, "Robert, let go." I let go of the kid, and the two left. I told my sergeant thanks for the warning. He said that next time there would be no warning. I was angry at the kid for what he did to his mother, but I wasn't going to hit him (although in my mind, I did right then and there).

I remembered these events throughout my career. As I have mentioned, my walk was weak for a good part of my career. I didn't attend church or read the Bible. Yet I was provided wisdom when I didn't ask for it. I did not always ask the Lord for guidance. When I did not ask, I got into trouble. I am so thankful that God listened, chose me, and wanted me to know his Son so I may obtain eternal life through the Word!

> *But when the Father sends the Advocate as my representative—that is, the Holy Spirit—he will teach you everything and will remind you of everything I have told you. I am leaving you with a gift—peace of mind and heart. And the peace I give is a gift the world cannot give. So, don't be troubled or afraid.*
> —John 14:26–27

> *Your word is a lamp for my feet, a light on my path. I have taken an oath and confirmed it, that I will follow your righteous laws.*
> —Psalms 119:105–106

> *So, I say, let the Holy Spirit guide your lives. Then you won't be doing what your sinful nature craves.*
> —Galatians 5:16

Slander

Slander is one of the most frequent trials that we contend with. Our human nature forces us to speak whatever is in our hearts and on our minds. If we do not have Christ leading us, our verbal and physical responses cannot be as God wants.

But my enemies say nothing but evil about me. "How soon will he die and be forgotten?" they ask. They visit me as if they were my friends, but all the while they gather gossip, and when they leave, they spread it everywhere. All who hate me whisper about me, imagining the worst. "He has some fatal disease," they say. "He will never get out of that bed!" Even my best friend, the one I trusted completely, the one who shared my food, has turned against me.
—Psalms 41:5–9

Slander and libel are nearly synonymous, as both deal with defamation. Slander deals with the verbal condemnation upon a person's character, while libel is a written or documentable attack. I'll refer to both slander and libel as "slander."

The *Merriam-Webster Dictionary* defines *slander* as

1: the utterance of false charges or misrepresentations which defame and damage another's reputation

2: a false and defamatory oral statement about a person.

The *Merriam-Webster Dictionary* defines *libel* as

1a: a written statement in which a plaintiff in certain courts sets forth the cause of action or the relief sought

b: archaic : a handbill especially attacking or defaming someone

2a: a written or oral defamatory statement or representation that conveys an unjustly unfavorable impression b(1): a statement or representation published without just cause and tending to expose another to public contempt.

There are also statues that cover slander and libel. California Civil Code Section 45 covers libel:

Libel is a false and unprivileged publication by writing, printing, picture, effigy, or other fixed representation to the eye, which exposes any person to hatred, contempt, ridicule, or obloquy, or which causes him to be shunned or avoided, or which has a tendency to injure him in his occupation.

California Civil Code Section 46 covers slander:

Slander is a false and unprivileged publication, orally uttered, and also communications by radio or any mechanical or other means which:

1. Charges any person with crime, or with having been indicted, convicted, or punished for crime;

2. Imputes in him the present existence of an infectious, contagious, or loathsome disease;

3. Tends directly to injure him in respect to his office, profession, trade or business, either by imputing to him general disqualification in those respects which the office or other occupation peculiarly requires, or by imputing something with reference to his office, profession, trade, or business that has a natural tendency to lessen its profits;

4. Imputes to him impotence or a want of chastity; or

5. Which, by natural consequence, causes actual damage.

We need to test what is being told to us. People spreading slander use the defaming comments to gain an emotional response from the listener. For this reason, we need to test what is being told to us. Just because a candidate we like gives their opinion, we can't take their statements as truth without research.

> *Wise people think before they act; fools don't—and even brag about their foolishness. An unreliable messenger stumbles into trouble, but a reliable messenger brings healing.*
> —Proverbs 13:16–17

In Acts 19, Demetrius the silversmith saw how Christianity was negatively impacting his business of making shrines to the goddess Artemis. He stirred up the crowd, which led to a large riot and the near-lynching of two of Paul's companions. The mayor became involved, accusing the mob of acting rashly and creating a situation in which the Romans would be called in to quell the disturbance.

War Stories

I worked with a partner whom I was told would throw me under the bus the first chance he got. I told the people telling me about him that I would make up my own mind. A few months later, as I walked into the station after filing some cases in court, I saw one of my informants speaking with my partner. I asked my partner what was going on. He said that my informant gave him the location of a rifle that was used in a recent gang murder and that several deputies were searching for the weapon.

I asked my partner if the informant had asked for assistance regarding his Section 8 housing. He said yes. I told him that the informant had been begging me to get him bumped up the Section 8 list for about a month. I asked my partner why didn't he call or page me. He said nothing. I told him that he had stolen my informant so he could get credit for solving a murder. He got red in the face, looked down, and said yes.

There was also a small command post set up for this incident, manned by my sergeant and monitored by my captain. A few minutes later, a deputy came in with a rifle that he said he found in a field where my informant had stated. The rifle was old and rusted, and had probably been in the field since the 1965 Watts Riots, twenty-five years earlier.

The sergeant and captain looked at the rifle and called my partner into the sergeant's office for a chat that lasted about twenty minutes. My partner came out red-faced and looking extremely embarrassed. Everyone knew what he had done for his own glory. I told him that if he had called or paged me before the extensive search, I would have told him that the informant just wanted us to intercede on his behalf of his Section 8.

Although I was told defaming comments about my partner by other deputies, I had to make up my own mind about him. In the end, the other deputies were right. He was a good detective, much better than I, but not a team player. He was not remorseful or apologetic. I worked with him for another year but was very wary in my dealings with him.

If we are victims of slander, we must let it roll off our backs. Only you and God know if what is being said is true. Jesus gave us examples on how to handle being a victim of slander. Peter and Paul followed Jesus's example:

> But when the leading priests and the elders made their
> accusations against him, Jesus remained silent. "Don't
> you hear all these charges they are bringing against
> you?" Pilate demanded. But Jesus made no response
> to any of the charges, much to the governor's surprise.
> (Matt. 27:12–14)

He did not retaliate when he was insulted, nor threaten revenge when he suffered. He left his case in the hands of God, who always judges fairly. (1 Pet. 2:23)

We bless those who curse us. We are patient with those who abuse us. We appeal gently when evil things are said about us. (1 Cor. 4:12–13)

Stand Tall

Many of the biblical examples of slander deal with sedition, the act of defiance or insurrection against the government. This is true. In fact, Jesus did come to overthrow the Satan-ruled governments of the world.

> *Don't imagine that I came to bring peace to the earth! I came not to bring peace, but a sword. "I have come to set a man against his father, a daughter against her mother, and a daughter-in-law against her mother-in-law. Your enemies will be right in your own house-hold!"*
> —Matthew 10:34–36

Jesus was only given over to the Jews after appealing to Pilate's loyalty to Caesar. In each of the four Gospels, Pilate only cared about his own position and public loyalty to Caesar. He showed no concern about the other accusations such as taxes, nor did Jesus deny his Kingship, a seditious act. In other words, Pilate only cared about self-survival.

> *Then Pilate tried to release him, but the Jewish leaders shouted, "If you release this man, you are no 'friend of Caesar.' Anyone who declares himself a king is a rebel against Caesar."*
> —John 19:12

War Stories

In my last assignment, I handled contracts with private security companies. One company was owned and run by two former law enforcement executives. This company continually violated the terms of the contract and expected my agency to look the other way and allow the violations to continue because they were former law enforcement officers. For more than two years, I documented the violations via letters and worked with this company to help them overcome their deficiencies, but the company did not correct itself. Eventually, I told the company that they were going to be removed from their contracts.

The owners then sent a scathing letter to the sheriff making bogus accusations against me and appealing to the law enforcement bond between the sheriff and themselves. As my dad would say, "They called me everything but a gentleman." Along with my commander (and my documentation), I got called into the division chief's office for a meeting with the owners of the company. The owners were shocked that I was present; however, they began accusing me of bankrupting their company and having a personal bias against them. I did not say a word unless I was asked. I didn't need to. I knew what they were saying was bogus, as did my commander.

After the division chief gave them a politically correct rebuke, the owners couldn't have been nicer to me. In fact, after I retired, they asked me to be general manager and run the day-to-day operation of their business—which I respectfully declined. Actually, I felt bad for them. They were in over their heads and in financial trouble.

> *And now, dear brothers and sisters, one final thing.*
> *Fix your thoughts on what is true, and honorable, and*
> *right, and pure, and lovely, and admirable. Think about*
> *things that are excellent and worthy of praise. Keep*
> *putting into practice all you learned and received from*
> *me—everything you heard from me and saw me doing.*
> *Then the God of peace will be with you.*
> —Philippians 4:8–9

*Let your conversation be gracious and attractive so
that you will have the right response for everyone.*
—Colossians 4:6

Lying

Slander also includes deception and lying. We lie for a myriad of reasons.
Sometimes, we want to hide the truth, as Cain did when God asked where
Abel was: "Afterward the Lord asked Cain, 'Where is your brother?
Where is Abel?' 'I don't know,' Cain responded. 'Am I my brother's
guardian?'" (Gen. 4:9).

We may lie out of hate to make sure someone is punished. The
Pharisees made up multiple lies to Pilate about Jesus when they did not
get their way:

> They began to state their case: "This man has been
> leading our people astray by telling them not to pay
> their taxes to the Roman government and by claiming
> he is the Messiah, a king."
>
> So, Pilate asked him, "Are you the king of the Jews?"
> Jesus replied, "You have said it." Pilate turned to the
> leading priests and to the crowd and said, "I find noth-
> ing wrong with this man!"
>
> Then they became insistent. "But he is causing riots by
> his teaching wherever he goes—all over Judea, from
> Galilee to Jerusalem!" (Luke 23:2–5)

Lies are told to avoid keeping our word:

> "All right, go ahead," Pharaoh replied. "I will let you go
> into the wilderness to offer sacrifices to the Lord your
> God. But don't go too far away. Now hurry and pray

> for me." Moses answered, "As soon as I leave you, I
> will pray to the Lord, and tomorrow the swarms of flies
> will disappear from you and your officials and all your
> people. But I am warning you, Pharaoh, don't lie to us
> again and refuse to let the people go to sacrifice to the
> Lord." (Exod. 8:28–29)

Lies are told out of self-righteousness or greed. This is common in politics, including office politics. In these lies, people sell themselves out, often at the sake of friends and family:

> They betray their friends for their own advantage, so let
> their children faint with hunger. (Job 17:5)

> When you pray, don't be like the hypocrites who love
> to pray publicly on street corners and in the synagogues
> where everyone can see them. I tell you the truth, that is
> all the reward they will ever get. (Matt. 6:5)

> What sorrow awaits you Pharisees! For you love to sit in
> the seats of honor in the synagogues and receive re-
> spectful greetings as you walk in the marketplaces. Yes,
> what sorrow awaits you! For you are like hidden graves
> in a field. People walk over them without knowing the
> corruption they are stepping on. (Luke 11:43–44)

It is easy to see examples of this type of slander around election time. Candidates bring up any negative issue about their opponent they can find. To top it off, the candidate making the accusation ends the message with, "I support the content of this message."

Check out any social media site. It is full of groups in which people share a common interest. Many of these interests are based upon slander. People read the entries in these groups, become emotional about a particular issue, and pass on the slanderous or inaccurate information, which then goes worldwide.

We are no exception. Cops gossip more than any other group that I know of—yours truly included. Gossip among our peers may occur if we get passed over for a coveted position or a promotion. We may become jealous and often end up hating the person receiving the coveted position or promotion. This commonly leads to slander about this person, which spreads like wildfire, both at the facility where the person is currently stationed and at their new assignment. Usually the reason a person did not the job or promotion they wanted was because he or she did not score high enough or have the experience required.

When I started in law enforcement, I didn't get caught up in the petty goings-on of other deputies. Yet after a few years, I found myself listening to the crap others were saying, and I started spewing some of the garbage about others as well. After realizing what I had become, I changed my ways through God's help. I've gotten much better, but I cannot say I'm 100 percent yet. I keep on trying with the Lord's help.

Some lies we tell are half-truths designed to deflect guilt away from us.

> *Then the brothers killed a young goat and dipped
> Joseph's robe in its blood. They sent the beautiful robe
> to their father with this message: "Look at what we
> found. Doesn't this robe belong to your son?" Their fa-
> ther recognized it immediately. "Yes," he said, "it is my
> son's robe. A wild animal must have eaten him. Joseph
> has clearly been torn to pieces!"*
> —Genesis 37:31–33

As mentioned before, deception was the greatest act of evil and committed by Satan, the deceiver:

> The serpent was the shrewdest of all the wild animals
> the Lord God had made. One day he asked the woman,

"Did God really say you must not eat the fruit from any
of the trees in the garden?" "Of course, we may eat fruit
from the trees in the garden," the woman replied. "It's
only the fruit from the tree in the middle of the garden
that we are not allowed to eat. God said, 'You must not
eat it or even touch it; if you do, you will die.'"

"You won't die!" the serpent replied to the woman.
"God knows that your eyes will be opened as soon as
you eat it, and you will be like God, knowing both good
and evil." The woman was convinced. (Gen. 3:4–6)

Righteous Deception

Although we have been taught that all lying is wrong, there have been
some instances in the Bible where God used deceit accomplish his purpose. We are not to question the wisdom of God.

*Since God in his wisdom saw to it that the world would
never know him through human wisdom, he has used
our foolish preaching to save those who believe. It is
foolish to the Jews, who ask for signs from heaven. And
it is foolish to the Greeks, who seek human wisdom.
So, when we preach that Christ was crucified, the Jews
are offended and the Gentiles say it's all nonsense.
But to those called by God to salvation, both Jews and
Gentiles, Christ is the power of God and the wisdom of
God. This foolish plan of God is wiser than the wisest of
human plans, and God's weakness is stronger than the
greatest of human strength.*
—1 Corinthians 1:21–25

Abraham deceived two different kings, telling them that Sarah was
his sister. When the kings found out about Abraham's lies, they were

about to be punished by God. When the kings pleaded with God, God relented. He did not punish them because they were innocent, not having yet touched Sarah. In fact, Sarah was Abraham's half sister. Had God not allowed the deception, one of the kings would have taken Sarah as his own, and God's plan of salvation for us as descendants of Abraham through faith would not have occurred.

Jacob and Esau were twins, with Esau coming out first and inheriting the blessing of the firstborn. Esau sold his birthright to Jacob for a bowl of stew. When it came time for their father (Isaac) to give Esau his blessing, their mother (Rebecca) dressed Jacob in his brother's clothes and sent him to Isaac. When Isaac asked Jacob if he was Esau, Jacob said yes and received the blessing through deception. This fulfilled God's promise.

The sons in your womb will become two nations. From the very beginning, the two nations will be rivals. One nation will be stronger than the other; and your older son will serve your younger son.
—Genesis 25:23

Jesus's lineage to the tribe of Judah goes through Perez. Tamar, Judah's daughter-in-law, wanted to continue the lineage of Judah. She had been married to Judah's two oldest sons, but were both killed by the Lord. Judah promised her his youngest son when he became of age. However, Judah did not make good on his promise. Tamar deceived Judah, a widower, by dressing as a prostitute and becoming pregnant, giving birth to Perez. Judah admitted his error:

"Judah recognized them immediately and said, 'She is more righteous than I am, because I didn't arrange for her to marry my son Shelah.' And Judah never slept with Tamar again" (Gen. 38:26).

However, God's plan was that the Messiah was to be from the tribe of Judah. With two sons already dead and Judah not giving Shelah to Tamar, God had to act or make a commanding decision. God ensured that scripture was fulfilled just as he promised, with Jesus coming from the tribe of Judah.

Judah, your brothers will praise you. You will grasp your enemies by the neck. All your relatives will bow before you. Judah, my son, is a young lion that has finished eating its prey. Like a lion he crouches and lies down; like a lioness—who dares to rouse him? The scepter will not depart from Judah, nor the ruler's staff from his descendants, until the coming of the one to whom it belongs, the one whom all nations will honor.
—Genesis 49:8–10

In Joshua 2, Rahab saved the two scouts sent by Joshua to Jericho. She was asked by the king if the two men were with her. She said yes but lied and said they left the city as the gate was about to close. They were actually hidden in stalks of flax on her roof. The Lord used the deceit of Rahab, a prostitute, to further his plan to deliver Israel to his people, with Jericho being the first step.

In 2 Kings 10, Jehu called all the worshipers of Baal under the guise that he would worship Baal as Ahab had. He specifically said that no worshipper of God was to attend the service. In reality, Jehu assembled all worshippers of Baal and slaughtered them. The temple of Baal became a toilet. God doesn't play! It is stated in 2 Kings 10:27: "They smashed the sacred pillar and wrecked the temple of Baal, converting it into a public toilet, as it remains to this day."

Paul also used righteous deception and admitted doing so in his letters: "But be it so, I did not burden you: nevertheless, being crafty, I caught you with guile" (2 Cor. 12:16, Geneva Study Bible).

We also use deceit or lying to accomplish our authorized and legal law enforcement duties. As I've mentioned before, I acted as a seventeen-year old high school student when I was really a twenty-three-year-old deputy sheriff. The reason for the deceit was to remove drugs from a high school campus and make that a safer school.

War Stories

My partner and I were called to handle a call in a city out of our jurisdiction. The call was about a man who was under the influence of meth and was very violent. He was also a multidegree black belt in one of the martial arts. We responded to the location, which was his dojo.

The guy was whacked out. His pupils were blown out, his speech was 100 miles per hour, and he was paranoid and extremely jittery. He was afraid to leave his dojo, saying that the local police were going to kill him. He looked like a meth freak in a training film come to life. Because he was a definite a threat to his own safety, we had to take him in.

After a few minutes, I pointed out a random car in the parking lot and told the guy that the car was an undercover vehicle from the local police and that they were trying to kill him. This was why the sheriff's department came to protect him.

I said that I'd put cuffs on him so he appeared to be in our custody. When we arrived at our station, I would remove the cuffs and he could go. However, I had to treat the event like a real arrest, or the local police would take him from us. I told him I had to call my station and advise them because we were in another city's jurisdiction. He bought it!

Before we left the dojo, my partner called the watch commander and told him of the situation. When we arrived at the station, personnel were ready. He was arrested, booked, and held. He was not happy, but no one was hurt.

Yeah, I lied. But it was the only way to bring the suspect in safely. We could not leave the suspect at his location. As a martial arts master, this guy could have thumped both my partner and me before we could get our weapons drawn. However, it was not the day for any of us to die. I firmly believe that the hand of God was on all of us that day. He put the plan to solve the situation into my head and the words into my mouth via the Holy Spirit. I guess the survival prayer that I said each day at the beginning shift was heard by the Lord: "Help me treat everyone like I wanted to be treated, and let me go home in one piece."

Detectives use ruses or lies to get suspects to confess. Some think this is wrong, but if the lie is not done for personal gain, does not violate any state rules, and does not promise leniency or go against what Jesus taught—we do it. We are obligated to protect the public.

War Stories

I assisted a detective in interviewing an adult man who'd had sex with a girl under fourteen. The suspect spoke only Spanish. I told the suspect that while sex with a young girl may be legal in is country, it was illegal in the United States. While he did not overtly confess, he said that he did not know it was illegal. I knew he was lying, but I played along. I told him that if convicted, he could get many years in prison and may be deported to finish his sentence in a prison in his country. He asked me what to do. I told him the best thing to do is to tell the truth. He confessed. He could have been sentenced to a maximum of eight years, which was true. However, we were not going to send him to his home country to finish his sentence, but he did not know that.

Acting

An issue I want to bring up in this area is acting. As law enforcement officers, we must be the consummate actors. Our ability to convince others of the role we are playing or the ruse being used is critical in convicting or exonerating a suspect.

Additionally, those officers who go undercover place their own safety at risk to keep our communities safe. While I have never gone deep undercover to infiltrate a criminal enterprise, I have bought drugs in a few bars and was followed by drug dealer afterward to see if I was an undercover narcotics officer. It was a little unnerving. Undercover officers face some type of safety risk every day. If the officer is married or has children, this risk also includes his or her family. I have always said that professional actors do not face life-threatening stress or safety issues because of their profession.

Paul knew the need to be the consummate actor in order to bring people to Jesus. Each of his letters were written for a specific audience with a message of encouragement, guidance, or rebuking:

> Even though I am a free man with no master, I have become a slave to all people to bring many to Christ. When I was with the Jews, I lived like a Jew to bring the Jews to Christ. When I was with those who follow the Jewish law, I too lived under that law. Even though I am not subject to the law, I did this so I could bring to Christ those who are under the law.

> When I am with the Gentiles who do not follow the Jewish law, I too live apart from that law so I can bring them to Christ. But I do not ignore the law of God; I obey the law of Christ. When I am with those who are weak, I share their weakness, for I want to bring the weak to Christ. Yes, I try to find common ground with everyone, doing everything I can to save some. I do everything to spread the Good News and share in its blessings. (1 Cor. 9:10–23)

Paul demonstrated his ability to be all things to all men in his verbal dealings as well. He circumcised Timothy (whose mother was a Jew) to appeal to Jews, but did not circumcise Titus, who was Greek:

> In deference to the Jews of the area, he arranged for Timothy to be circumcised before they left, for everyone knew that his father was a Greek. Then they went from town to town, instructing the believers to follow the decisions made by the apostles and elders in Jerusalem. So, the churches were strengthened in their faith and grew larger every day. (Acts 16:3–5)

And they supported me and did not even demand that my companion Titus be circumcised, though he was a Gentile. Even that question came up only because of some so-called believers there—false ones, really—who were secretly brought in. They sneaked in to spy on us and take away the freedom we have in Christ Jesus. They wanted to enslave us and force us to follow their Jewish regulations.

But we refused to give in to them for a single moment. We wanted to preserve the truth of the gospel message for you. (Gal. 2:3–5)

In Acts 17, Paul addressed a group of Greek philosophers, focusing on their worship of false idols. In Acts 18, he appealed to Jewish customs. Both instances resulted in many persons turning to Christ. In other words, he used reason when dealing with Gentiles and law in working with the Jews.

I was walking along I saw your many shrines. And one of your altars had this inscription on it: "To an Unknown God." This God, whom you worship without knowing, is the one I'm telling you about.
—Acts 17:23

Paul stayed in Corinth for some time after that, then said good-bye to the brothers and sisters and went to nearby Cenchrea. There he shaved his head according to Jewish custom, marking the end of a vow.
—Acts 18:18

Go with them to the Temple and join them in the purification ceremony, paying for them to have their heads ritually shaved. Then everyone will know that the

*rumors are all false and that you yourself observe the
Jewish laws.*
—Acts 21:24

Many people did not understand the differences in Paul's actions and
letters, including yours truly until I studied the Bible.

*This is what our beloved brother Paul also wrote to
you with the wisdom God gave him—speaking of these
things in all of his letters. Some of his comments are
hard to understand, and those who are ignorant and
unstable have twisted his letters to mean something
quite different, just as they do with other parts of
Scripture. And this will result in their destruction.*
—2 Peter 3:15–16

David's adviser and friend, Hushai, did a great acting job:

Return to Jerusalem and tell Absalom, "I will now be
your adviser, O king, just as I was your father's adviser in the past." Then you can frustrate and counter
Ahithophel's advice. Zadok and Abiathar, the priests,
will be there. Tell them about the plans being made
in the king's palace, and they will send their sons
Ahimaaz and Jonathan to tell me what is going on. So,
David's friend Hushai returned to Jerusalem, getting
there just as Absalom arrived. (2 Sam. 15:34–37)

When David's friend Hushai the Arkite arrived, he went
immediately to see Absalom. "Long live the king!" he
exclaimed. "Long live the king!" "Is this the way you
treat your friend David?" Absalom asked him. "Why
aren't you with him?"

> "I'm here because I belong to the man who is chosen by
> the Lord and by all the men of Israel," Hushai replied.
> "And anyway, why shouldn't I serve you? Just as I was
> your father's adviser, now I will be your adviser!" (2
> Sam. 16:16–19)

Absalom discounted the advice of his adviser, Ahithophel, and listened to the bogus advice of Hushai. As a result of Hushai's loyalty to David through acting, David's life was spared and his throne restored.

On the other hand, if we know that a crime did not occur as it was documented in a crime report, we have the obligation to protect the suspect from false prosecution.

War Stories

As a detective, I received a rape case with a school police officer and five gang members as suspects. The case got some media attention. When I tried to contact the victim, I learned that she had fled to San Francisco. I thought this was strange, so I asked the arresting deputy why she would flee. He said that she was probably afraid of retaliation. I then spoke with the suspects separately. They all said basically the same thing. The gang members remembered the school police officer, who was off duty, from their high school days. The six of them had a few beers and went to a location frequented by prostitutes to purchase sex. The victim was a prostitute who was upset that she did not get paid in full for her services. I spoke again with the arresting deputy. He denied what the suspects had told me.

After a couple of days, I was able to speak with the victim. She confirmed what the six suspects told me, saying that the deputy told her what to say. She refused to come back to Los Angeles, did not want to prosecute, and wanted no part in the case. By this time, the district attorney and my captain were getting a bit anxious as to why the case had not yet been filed. I told them that I was having difficulty getting the victim to testify. In no way was I going to file the case. After about a week, I advised the district attorney and my captain that the victim would not come back to Los Angeles. The two agreed to let the case drop. The six were released.

I had known the arresting deputy for over ten years at that point. I knew that he had walked a gray line in some of his previous arrests, but never to the degree of an out-and-out lie, as was the rape.

I ripped him a new one! I discussed the case with my sergeant; we agreed to let the incident lie. We had just taken over a new high-profile contract, and a scandal like this would have ridiculed the department. The arresting officer transferred to another station at his first opportunity. A prostitute had more integrity than a sworn law enforcement officer. Never judge a book by its cover.

> *The words of the wicked are like a murderous ambush,*
> *but the words of the godly save lives.*
> —Proverbs 12:6

Although I try, I do not consider myself godly. I just try to follow what is right by the Lord.

CHAPTER 4:
Apathy

Remember, it is sin to know what you ought to do and then not do it.
—James 4:17

The *Merriam-Webster Dictionary* defines *apathy* as

1: lack of feeling or emotion : IMPASSIVENESS, drug abuse leading to apathy and depression

2: lack of interest or concern : INDIFFERENCE, political apathy

Initially I thought that apathy was burnout or giving up. However, I learned that apathy is also fence sitting, where we fail to commit to an issue, either pro or con. After realizing the true meaning of apathy, I understood the following verse: "I know all the things you do, that you are neither hot nor cold. I wish that you were one or the other! But since you are like lukewarm water, neither hot nor cold, I will spit you out of my mouth!" (Rev. 3:15–16)

And this one: "Wake up! Strengthen what little remains, for even what is left is almost dead. I find that your actions do not meet the requirements of my God. Go back to what you heard and believed at first; hold to it firmly. Repent and turn to me again. If you don't wake up, I will come to you suddenly, as unexpected as a thief" (Rev. 3:2–3).

Although these verses were written over two thousand years ago, they show that Jesus is giving an advanced warning about apathy and what happens when don't conduct ourselves as Christians. If we have strayed, he wants to give us every opportunity to recommit ourselves to God and keep the gift of eternal life that he promised to us.

With all that we see or deal with in careers, it is understandable that we become complacent at times. Many of us enter our careers with a fervent desire to help others. However, after years of solving other people's problems or having domestic issues at home because we work too many hours or are exhausted, we lose that passion. We tend to just go through the motions with little or no feeling for those we serve.

> *I will search with lanterns in Jerusalem's darkest corners to punish those who sit complacent in their sins. They think the Lord will do nothing to them, either good or bad. So, their property will be plundered, their homes will be ransacked. They will build new homes but never live in them. They will plant vineyards but never drink wine from them. That terrible day of the Lord is near. Swiftly it comes—a day of bitter tears, a day when even strong men will cry out. It will be a day when the Lord 's anger is poured out—a day of terrible distress and anguish, a day of ruin and desolation, a day of darkness and gloom, a day of clouds and blackness.*
> —Zephaniah 1:12–15

It is difficult to maintain or rekindle that passion without some type of incentive that motivates us. We may have been placed in a boring work detail or assigned to work in an area that we detest. In order not let the job beat us up, we need to make the best of what we perceive as a bad situation.

We may be assigned to a module in the jail where inmates with a certain type of behavior that we can't stand are housed. Years later when we come across people with the same type behavior in our personal or professional life, we will know how to deal with them in a respectful manner.

While assigned to a location you don't like, you continue to do your job without complaint. A supervisor notices your professionalism and remembers you years later when you interview with him for a job you want. He hires you because of how you handled yourself.

You are assigned to a location you don't like as a supervisor and continue to do your job without complaint. The officers under you will notice this. You will gain their respect and unwittingly become a positive role model for them and the officers whom they will supervise. Your actions will continue to have a positive impact long after you retire.

The driving force for the rekindling of our spirit during these times is the Lord. If we listen to him, he will inspire a new enthusiasm for our jobs and our lives.

We need to understand that wherever we have been placed, we will be given the opportunity to make a difference in someone's life, either in a positive or negative way—hopefully in a positive way. We may unknowingly impact someone's life just by how we conduct ourselves, or we may knowingly impact someone's life by sharing the Word. How we positively influence others is based upon the gifts that we have been given by the Holy Spirit. Any negative behavior that we impart is a form of apathy and comes from Satan via our human nature of sin.

In addition to maintaining our passion and sustaining our motivation, situations we handle are trials that can cause great stress and often deep depression. How many people have to take someone's life or see a violent crime scene that defies definition? Who works for years in the confines of a jail or prison where you are subjected to constant negativity by inmates whose entire life is based upon criminal acts and would jump at the chance to slit your throat? How many professions train you to work with people who, for the most part, hate you, mock you, and persecute you simply because you want to help them?

Many of the things we will see or have to do in our careers go beyond normal human understanding. Our chosen profession affords us a daily opportunity to go beyond our human fragilities and place our trust in Jesus, who experienced and overcame all of our human weaknesses.

> *That is why we never give up. Though our bodies are dying, our spirits are being renewed every day. For our present troubles are small and won't last very long. Yet they produce for us a glory that vastly outweighs them and will last forever! So, we don't look at the troubles we can see now; rather, we fix our gaze on things that cannot be seen. For the things we see now will soon be gone, but the things we cannot see will last forever.*
> —2 Corinthians 4:16–18

> *The faithful love of the Lord never ends! His mercies never cease. Great is his faithfulness; his mercies begin afresh each morning.*
> —Lamentations 3:22–23

> *Never be lazy, but work hard and serve the Lord enthusiastically. Rejoice in our confident hope. Be patient in trouble, and keep on praying.*
> —Romans 12:11–12

Uninhibited

Per the *Oxford Dictionary*, the definition of *uninhibited* is: "behaving or expressing yourself freely without worrying about what other people think."

The *Merriam-Webster Dictionary* defines *uninhibited* as:

: free from inhibition

uninhibited exuberance

: boisterously informal

a festive uninhibited party

To maintain our zeal as Christians, we need to be uninhibited in our faith. The Bible lists many examples of being uninhibited in demonstrating their love of God.

David

In 2 Samuel, David was more than overjoyed to establish a permanent home for the Ark of the Covenant in Jerusalem, and he showed his joy by dancing and leaping in an ephod, a priestly vestment. His wife, Michal, told him that as king of Israel, he looked foolish dancing in religious clothing.

As the daughter of the previous king, Saul, she was jealous of David's fame at the sake of her father. She slanderously berated David, accusing him of being vulgar and half naked in order to impress his slave girls. However, David rebuked her, stating that he was dancing for the Lord and was willing to look even more foolish and to suffer more humiliation for the Lord. As a result of her behavior, she bore no children.

But as the Ark of the Lord entered the City of David, Michal, the daughter of Saul, looked down from her window. When she saw King David leaping and dancing before the Lord, she was filled with contempt for him.
—2 Samuel 6:16

When David returned home to bless his own family, Michal, the daughter of Saul, came out to meet him. She said in disgust, "How distinguished the king of Israel

looked today, shamelessly exposing himself to the ser-
vant girls like any vulgar person might do!"

David retorted to Michal, "I was dancing before the
Lord, who chose me above your father and all his fam-
ily! He appointed me as the leader of Israel, the people
of the Lord, so I celebrate before the Lord. Yes, and I
am willing to look even more foolish than this, even to
be humiliated in my own eyes! But those servant girls
you mentioned will indeed think I am distinguished!"
So, Michal, the daughter of Saul, remained childless
throughout her entire life.
—2 Samuel 6:20–23

Isaiah

In Isaiah 20:2, Isaiah walked around naked and barefoot for three years. He freely expressed the uninhibited or reckless love and obedience that he had for God. This act required great faith, as public nudity and naked-ness have been described as sin since the book of Genesis.

According to the book of Genesis, being naked was looked upon as sin. In Genesis 9, Noah shows his anger toward his son Ham when he saw Noah naked. He called his brothers, who covered their naked father while averting their eyes. Noah woke up and learned that Ham saw him naked, and then cursed Ham's son Canaan. However, he blessed his other sons, who had averted their eyes.

In Genesis 3, Adam told God that he was hiding because he and Eve were naked. Adam learned that he was naked only after sinning by eat-ing the Forbidden Fruit. Adam and Eve went from being uninhibited in God's love to being repressed in sin.

Hosea

God directed Hosea to marry a prostitute, Gomer. Although Gomer was prostituting herself, the Lord told Hosea to buy his wife back to redeem her. Hosea did as commanded. For Hosea to take his adulterous wife back from her public life as a prostitute required the free and public display of Hosea's trust and uninhibited love of the Lord.

Prostitutes have mostly been portrayed as sinful, deceitful, and wicked. This goes for both male and female prostitutes, as there were male shrine prostitutes. Gomer is one of three prostitutes who have been specifically noted in the Bible. She was not cast in a positive light. The Lord used the relationship of Hosea and Gomer as a sign of his unrelenting and uninhibited love of Israel. Like Israel, Gomer would come back to Hosea when she needed him, and not because she truly loved him. The other two prostitutes described in the Bible, Rahab and Mary Magdalene, are described as heroines for their faith in God.

Mary Magdalene

Speaking of Mary Magdalene, she showed a great uninhibited love of Jesus. She is described as a sinful woman or a prostitute from whom Jesus had cast out a demon. It is believed that she is the woman who washed Jesus's feet with her tears and the woman whom Jesus saved from stoning. However, it is documented that she was with Jesus at the Trial by Pilate, the Crucifixion, and the Resurrection. She was also the first to see Jesus after the Resurrection, who sent her to tell the apostles that he had risen.

What a field day the Pharisees and Sadducees must have had with this—a sinner following a blasphemer! Yet God used a sinful woman to proclaim to the world that Jesus had risen. This is another great example of mercy and redemption for those who believe in Jesus as the Messiah. She did not care what others thought. She was cleansed of her demons and saved. As is true of all plans set by Satan, it backfired. God used a sinner to show that he loves and accepts all of us. Mercy, and not rote obedience to a law, is what he desires. His plans are always true.

There is a song that my church sings, which I really like. I looked it up and saw that it is called "Reckless Love," written by Caleb Culver, Cory Asbury and Ran Jackson, and sung by Cory Asbury. This is the chorus:

> O, the overwhelming, never-ending, reckless love of
> God
>
> O, it chases me down, fights 'til I'm found, leaves the
> 99
>
> I couldn't earn it, and I don't deserve it, still, You give
> Yourself away
>
> O, the overwhelming, never-ending, reckless love of
> God, yeah.

This states that God so loved all of us that he is uninhibitedly or recklessly sent his Son to die for us. He leaves the ninety-nine (the self-righteous) and looks for the one (us sinners). The Father is not willing to let even one of his of flock perish (Matt. 18:12–14). *Reckless* does not mean careless or rash, but bold and forthright.

This verse, for me, sums up the term *uninhibited* for me: "The man answered, 'You must love the Lord your God with all your heart, all your soul, all your strength, and all your mind.' And, 'Love your neighbor as yourself'" (Luke 10:27).

If we do this, then we don't care what others think. We will have placed God as our priority, through obedience to Jesus: "If anyone is ashamed of me and my message in these adulterous and sinful days, the Son of Man will be ashamed of that person when he returns in the glory of his Father with the holy angels" (Mark 8:38).

Good Samaritan

Getting back to how this applies to our profession, we can't be afraid to take action. We must be bold and do what is right. Do not be afraid what people think if we want do our jobs correctly. We can draw a parallel to the story of the Good Samaritan to police work. A priest and then a Levite see an injured robbery victim in the road and ignore him. Only a despised Samaritan came to the aid of the robbery victim.

We may be the priest or Levite in our daily work life, when we fail to help the robbery victim (handle our duties). There may be a time when we are on our way back to the station and see a traffic accident. We drive by and ignore it. There may a time when a report is needed, but we talk our way out of the report because we don't want to write it. There may a crime that occurred in another station area or agency, but we refuse to handle the call, or we leave before the other station or agency arrives. In other words, we become apathetic or "kiss off" these duties.

There will also be times when we have to take physical action. This may be to protect the public or our partners. I've seen too many instances where partners freeze up or are afraid to take physical action. The result often ends up with an officer getting hurt.

War Stories

I had a situation where I was working overtime with a partner in a crowded mall during the Christmas season. A violent gang member who had walked away from a psychiatric hospital entered the mall and threatened to jump from the second floor. I called for backup (two deputies) and made a plan that we were going to take him down before he could jump. When I grabbed the subject, only my partner jumped in. My partner was an older, skinny watch deputy who had not worked the streets for over five years. The other two, a training officer and his trainee, refused to get involved because of the large crowd in the mall. One of the two deputies said, "Oh, man, we shouldn't have done that." After the incident, the four of us had debriefing. I ripped the training officer a new one for showing fear and giving his trainee a poor example. However, I gained a lot of respect for my partner, who had not been in a radio car for over five years. Thank the Lord, no one got hurt.

Another call I had was a hit-and-run where a four-year-old girl was the victim. When my partner (a trainee) and I arrived, I saw that she was dead. My partner said that he wanted to give CPR. I remembered the call of the family living in a chicken coop that I had handled as a trainee a few years earlier, and how angry I was that there was nothing that I could do. I also thought of the crash that I was involved in where a nine-year-old boy had died.

Although she was dead, we performed CPR on the little girl. I held the girl's jaw together while he gave breaths. The fire department responded in a few minutes, although it seemed like an eternity.

I was very proud of my partner's immediate and uninhibited act of compassion for the girl and her family. A trainee showed me one of the greatest acts of recklessness and boldness that I had witnessed throughout my career. I look back on this event now and realize that the Lord used this incident to help me fight some of the mental garbage that the two calls that I mentioned in the previous paragraph had put in my head. As I have mentioned, my walk was weak, yet God never abandoned me and continued to provide opportunities for me to get healed through Jesus.

Supervisors and Leaders

Although people are promoted to supervisor, it is difficult to *make* someone a good leader. Book learning, written tests, and oral interviews are good indicators that someone knows what is needed to be a good supervisor—but not a leader. When crunch time hits, some supervisors can't lead or make a decision to save their life. Out of fear or lack of confidence, or because they are control freaks, indecisive supervisors tend to be micromanagers in noncritical situations that they can control.

To be successful as a law enforcement officer or as a Christian, we must be leaders. Not all law enforcement supervisors or paid clergy are leaders, and not all leaders are law enforcement supervisors or paid clergy. A leader is a person who has a commanding influence or authority. Jesus himself was not a paid clergy, nor was John the Baptist, nor were Peter or Paul. Yet all were great leaders.

You will keep in perfect peace those whose minds are steadfast, because they trust in you.
—Isaiah 26:3

For the Lord will be at your side and will keep your foot from being snared.
—Proverbs 3:26

War Stories

As a sergeant, I responded to a call of a suicidal female (who only spoke Korean) with a gun at a high-end hotel. After speaking with the crisis negotiation team, she said that she would put the gun on the floor as the handling deputies and I entered then room. However, as we entered, we heard a gunshot and saw her turn toward us with the gun in her right hand.

Believing that she was in the act of "suicide by cop," I felt that she was shooting at us. As I was about to return fire, a deputy yelled out, "Bobby, don't shoot! She dropped the gun." I could not see her dropping the gun from my position. I did not shoot. The deputy was correct that she dropped the gun after shooting herself in the left shoulder. He saved her life. Had I shot her, the shooting would have been justified, although ultimately unnecessary.

I praise the Lord that he gave me the wisdom to be influenced and listen to someone with better knowledge of the situation than me. Oh, yeah, the deputy who saw the woman drop the gun also happens to be a believer.

Apathy via fear or reluctance to act can occur to supervisors and is referred to as "supervisor cowardice." I've seen this cowardice throughout my career as a deputy, sergeant, and lieutenant. It is not always easy to do what is right. Sometimes, you may have to manage your former radio car partner, or you are told by your supervisor to write a false performance evaluation on one of your subordinates.

You can't let personal sentiment or negative performance evaluation cloud your decisions. This has cost me a few friends over the years and cost me a few promotions. I've been removed from jobs because I refused to do things that go against what Jesus would do. When chastised for my actions, I would tell my supervisors that when I look in the mirror, I like what I see. I have never forgotten what I look like: an imperfect, never-quitting child of God: "For if you listen to the word and don't obey, it is like glancing at your face in a mirror. You see yourself, walk away, and forget what you look like" (James 1:23–24).

I mentioned supervisor cowardice. This cowardice may be the result of being overwhelmed or just plain laziness. Some officers, upon promotion, feel that they have worked hard to pass the promotion process and have earned the right to rest. Between performance evaluations, force incidents, citizen/inmate complaints, internal affairs investigations, and conducting mandated training, supervisors are busy.

Additionally, you catch grief when your paperwork is not completed on time. Paperwork is important, but I used to tell people that I worked with, "Monkeys can be trained to write paper." These mechanical or written portions of being a supervisor do not include the most important aspect of supervision or management: walking around and talking with your officers, public, and inmates. We used to call this MBWA: "management by walking around."

Supervisors should spend the majority of their time in the field and sporadically respond to calls for service or incidents within the jails. Supervisors need to be out there with their troops, hands-on. However, supervisors should not micromanage. Troops should be allowed to make their own decisions, whenever possible, with the guidance of their supervisor. How else will they learn?

When you see this huge workload, it is a normal response to metaphorically "curl up in a ball" and become lazy. This often leads your subordinates to make decisions that they should not make or to act unprofessionally because there is no one to guide them.

In LASD, custody is one of the more challenging assignments. Custody deputies are usually right out of the academy and ready to take on the world. These new deputies need strong supervision to keep them in line with departmental policy, as they usually aren't prepared for the reality of being in a confined environment and

- being surrounded by inmates who don't like the police.

- knowing that it may take years before they can transfer to a patrol station.

- being sick for the first month, as there is nearly every airborne illness known to man floating in the air system.

- having "John Wayne syndrome" combined with boredom.

Supervisors have their hands full. I did! Remember that idle hands are the tools of the devil.

War Stories

My first day as a supervisor was the first day of the Rodney King Riots in 1992. My facility consisted of wooden barracks, like on the television show *Hogan's Heroes*. The inmates rioted, burning down all the guard towers and damaging some of the barracks. Within hours, we had the National Guard conducting perimeter control, as many deputies were temporarily assigned to the streets. The inmate to staff ratio on the compound at this time was about 60:1. I was a brand-new baby-faced sergeant of thirty-two, with many deputies older than I. At times, I was also the watch commander.

As I sat in my car before the beginning of my first shift, I asked the Lord to let me and my deputies go home safely. I probably prayed this more fervently or stronger than I ever did as a patrol deputy. As I entered the watch sergeant's office, I was given a video camera and assigned nine or ten force investigations. About thirty minutes later, I called all my deputies together for a briefing and told them what I expected, as we were to conduct numerous inmate transfers. Many deputies were talking about doling out street justice on some inmates because of the riots. In the briefing, one deputy with about three months on asked me why he had to do a specific task. I told him, "Dude, usually I will ask you to do a specific task. But in rare instances, you will do what you are told because I said so. This is that rare instance. Do you understand?" No one else questioned my directives, nor did anyone else discuss street justice.

The deputies were outstanding! I made some good friends among those deputies. The deputies began to trust me, and a good working relationship with most of them began. Nothing in my life was as stressful as this period—a newly promoted sergeant, with an assignment eighty miles from home, and working 6pm to 6am during a major riot. Also, I was going through a divorce (and had my head in my rear end). However, these deputies looked out for me.

I needed the Lord and asked for help. Boy, did he answer! Knowing that patience is not my strong point, he answered my prayers *fast*. I started reading my Bible more frequently, relied on God's help more often, and started to feel better overall.

After a few days, I was able to take a deep breath and get a handle on force investigations. I look back now and thank the Lord that I was thrown into a "baptism of fire." I now could complete force investigations in my sleep and crank them out pretty fast. All the other supervisors and managers at this facility were much older than me, with many ready to retire. Although they were overwhelmed, they did not retreat to their office and were out on the compound with the troops. As neared my retirement twenty years after the riots, I recalled the positive actions of these supervisors and emulated them.

> *Trust in the Lord with all your heart and lean not on*
> *your own understanding; in all your ways submit to*
> *him, and he will make your paths straight.*
> —Proverbs 3:5–6

Commit to the Lord whatever you do, and he will establish your plans.
—Proverbs 16:3

But when you ask, you must believe and not doubt, because the one who doubts is like a wave of the sea, blown and tossed by the wind.
—James 1:6

The Lord is near to all who call on him, to all who call on him in truth.
—Psalms 145:18

We need to act as the Samaritan, and not the Levite or priest. We may be persecuted or hated for our profession or Christian belief, but we cannot let our natural inclinations or the actions of others dissuade us from our duties as a law enforcement officer or our fulfillment as Christians. We all answer to a much higher authority than the sheriff, police chief, or warden.

For the Lord your God is the God of gods and Lord of Lords. He is the great God, the mighty and awesome God, who shows no partiality and cannot be bribed.
—Deuteronomy 10:17

Now then, let the fear of the Lord be upon you. Be careful what you do, for there is no injustice with the Lord our God, or partiality or taking bribes.
—2 Chronicles 19:7

As we progress through our careers, we enter several chapters, both at work and home. Many of these events are joyous and uplifting, such as marriages, kids and grandkids, and promotions, and helping the public and planning retirement. However, many events are miserable and pessimistic, such as divorces, guilt from not being at home, infidelity, peer pressure, internal politics, and boredom. Negative events in our personal and professional lives are the events that scar us, causing stress and depression. These events can lead to alcoholism, drug addiction, and suicide. Satan uses the negative events in our lives as a foothold to disrupt our walk with the Lord.

Depression and Post-Traumatic Stress Syndrome (PTSD)

Depression and PTSD are not new twentieth or twenty-first century phenomena.

In 480 BC, Spartan commander Leonidas would rest his troops, as they were psychologically and emotionally spent from past battles.

By 1678, Swiss military physicians, some of the first medical professionals to recognize the symptoms and behaviors that characterize PTSD, used the term "nostalgia" to describe the condition.

During the Civil War it was called "soldier's heart" or "exhaustion."

In World War I, it was called "shell shock."

In World War II, it was "battle fatigue."

In the Vietnam era, it was called "Post-Vietnam Syndrome."

The Bible is full of people who suffered from depression and PTSD:

- David: Experienced many battles. Infant son died. Had guilt behind ordering the death of Bathsheba's husband in battle. Was sought out to be killed by Saul and Absalom.

- Elijah: Ran for fear of being killed by Jezebel after defeating the prophets of Baal. "I have had enough Lord, he said. Take my life, I am not better than my ancestors" (1 Kings 19:4).

- Jonah: After running from God, was given a second chance to preach in Nineveh. Instead of praising God, he asked God to kill him: "Now O Lord, take away my life, for it is better for me to die than to live" (Jon. 4:3).

- Moses: Disrespected by his own people, forced to flee Egypt, fought Pharaoh, and then dealt with the stiff-necked Israelites in the desert: "But now, please forgive their sin—but if not, then blot me out of the book you have written" (Exod. 32:32).

- Jeremiah: Constantly rejected and ridiculed by his own people. Forbidden to marry: "Cursed be the day I was born…why did I ever come out of the womb to see trouble and sorrow and to end my days in shame?" (Jer. 20:14, 18).

- Mark: The man in the tombs shrieking, crying, and cutting himself with stones, then praising God after the demons were expelled (Mark 5:2–20).

- Mary Magdalene being cured of the illnesses and seven demons (Luke 8:1–2). *Illness* and *demons* referred to mental health issues. With Luke being a doctor, he would have paid more attention and greater accuracy than the nonmedical Gospel writers. The number seven probably refers to completeness to show that Jesus completely cured her.

The common thread that all these persons in the Bible share is faith in our Father. Modern medicine is wonderful, but dependence it alone often leads to addiction. Total reliance on secular psychology takes us away from God. There is nothing wrong with medicine or psychology to help fight depression, but these are only aids. The only way to be completely healed is through Jesus. Use what God has provided through science as an aid and not a healer. Only God is the healer.

> *And everyone who calls on the name of the Lord will be saved.*
> —Acts 2:21

Whoever believes and is baptized will be saved, but whoever does not believe will be condemned.
—Mark 16:16

For it is with your heart that you believe and are justified, and it is with your mouth that you profess your faith and are saved.
—Romans 10:10

"Go," said Jesus, "your faith has healed you." Immediately he received his sight and followed Jesus along the road."
—Matthew 10:52

Evil One

Do you think that Satan would think twice about using science (human wisdom) to take us away from God? If he uses our weakness (depression) to get to us, why wouldn't he use science to strengthen his foothold in us?

Satan himself masquerades as an angel of light. It is not surprising, then, if his servants masquerade as servants of righteousness. Their end will correspond to their actions.
—2 Corinthians 11:14–15

You belong to your father, the devil, and you want to carry out your father's desire. He was a murderer from the beginning, not holding to the truth, for there is no truth in him. When he lies, he speaks his native language, for he is a liar and the father of lies.
—John 8:44

For the wisdom of this world is foolishness with God.
—1 Corinthians 3:19

All mankind is stupid, devoid of knowledge; Every gold-smith is put to shame by his idols, for his molten images are deceitful, and there is no breath in them.
—Jeremiah 51:17

I most definitely have suffered from depression, handling it in a human way. When my walk was weak, I found it difficult to handle certain aspects of the job. As stated previously, at times, I turned to alcohol. As I progressed through my career, my walk got stronger, yet there were more stressful situations in my life. I found it much easier to handle these situations. Instead of drinking, I resumed working out to "purge the demons."

Today, I hit the gym about five days a week. I listen to the Word or Christian music as I work out, and I wear a Christian T-shirt with a funny saying on it. I have dedicated my gym time 100 percent to the Lord. In turn, I've had a couple of fellow gym rats ask me about the Lord because of my shirts, and I've able to share a bit about our Savior. I realized that running is a gift from God that I use to this day to blow off steam and clear my head to make God-based decisions.

In addition to relieving stress, another benefit of working out for law enforcement officers is conditioning.

I had an instructor at Fullerton Community College in Fullerton, California, named Bob Smitson. He was an active Los Angeles Police Department sergeant assigned to the academy and taught police survival. He told us that one item that we could do to improve our chances of survival in officer-involved shootings or other critical incidents was physical conditioning.

When your body is good shape and functioning at a high level, you may have as much an additional pint of blood in your body, giving your body more time before bleeding out. I have always remembered this and told my peers and subordinates of this fact, and encouraged them to work out.

Also, being in good shape gives you a better chance to make your retirement last longer than the years that you worked, God willing. I love it when I see a retired deputy who worked for thirty years and enjoyed over thirty years of retirement!

People may say that we knew the job was dangerous when we took it, and that is true. Our training tries to prepare us for every situation or to be everything to everyone at all times. Only one person can be all things, to all people, at all times—and it is not any of us! However, we keep on trying. If our faith in Jesus Christ is not strong, we fall back on human methods to cope. The Lord will give us the strength to overcome these trials.

> *No temptation has overtaken you except what is common to mankind. And God is faithful; he will not let you be tempted beyond what you can bear. But when you are tempted, he will also provide a way out so that you can endure it.*
> —1 Corinthians 10:13

> *Be strong and courageous. Do not be afraid or terrified because of them, for the Lord your God goes with you; he will never leave you nor forsake you.*
> —Deuteronomy 31:6

> *I have told you these things, so that in me you may have peace. In this world you will have trouble. But take heart! I have overcome the world.*
> —John 16:33

> *If anyone serves, he should do it with the strength God provides, so that in all things God may be praised through Jesus Christ.*
> —1 Peter 4:11

In other words, the Lord will not give you more than you can a handle. If he has placed you in law enforcement, he will be there to guide you. This does not mean that fighting depression will be easy. But faith in Jesus Christ is the only way successfully fight this worldly emotion.

LASD has a psychological services bureau that department members and their families may use. I have used them on occasion; they are outstanding. In fact, one psychologist was an ardent Christian who helped me through my divorce and helped me improve my walk with the Lord. However, the services offered by the bureau often go unused for fear that the psychologist may report certain issues to the department member's superiors, or fear of the "John Wayne" stigma that you are weak if you see psychologist. Don't let your ego get in the way of helping yourself. You are loved by God and promised eternal life if you believe in Jesus. Like a new recruit, your department has made a major investment in you. As a Christian, God made the ultimate investment in you—the death of his Son.

Addiction

We handle situations or see things in our daily routine that permanently scar us:

- Solving people's problems when they are usually at their worst and don't want us there

- Going to a location and planning for worst-case scenario as we respond

- Facing a possible ambush or attack by one spouse when we arrest the other spouse

- Being a first responder to a horrendous crime scene

Imagine that you are off duty in thirty minutes, having a cup of coffee at your favorite doughnut shop, telling lies and other war stories to your peers. Just as you refill your cup, you receive a call of shots fired or of a multicar traffic accident with numerous injuries or some other major incident. Your coffee goes out the window, and you shift into cop mode. Your heart starts beating faster, and your blood pressure increases. You are coordinating the call on your radio and making decisions as you drive to the location. Once at the location, you immediately assess the situation, assign officers to complete tasks, and then ensure that the incident is correctly documented for either criminal prosecution or civil liability. Remember, less than five minutes ago, you were at the local donut shop with a cup ready to go home. My heart started revving as I wrote this paragraph; thank God I drink decaf now. I have to drink decaf now because of handling numerous stressful calls for service or jail incidents.

A March 30, 2018, article in *Psychology Today*[2] states that 20 to 25 percent of the national law enforcement community have either an alcohol or drug dependency issue, as compared to less than 10 percent for the general public. Reasons given in the article for the abuse are: job stress, rotating shift work (sleep deprivation), long hours, insular culture, the access to illicit drugs from narcotic arrests, and prescription drug abuse from the many injuries sustained throughout our career.

When I joined the LASD in 1982, marijuana was still a felony, and any drug use was subject to a candidate's disqualification. I had smoked marijuana in high school. My high school was like the one in the movie *Fast Times at Ridgemont High*: parties on Friday nights; drinking, drugs, and carousing were commonplace. Once I decided to become a law enforcement officer, I stopped smoking marijuana. There was a five-year period from the last time I smoked and when I interviewed with the LASD. When I told my friends that I stopped smoking because I wanted to be a law enforcement officer, they laughed at me and blew marijuana smoke in my face. Good friends, indeed!

When I met with my background investigator, who had my application in his hands, he asked me if I had ever done drugs. I told him yes and that it had been five years since I last had smoked marijuana. Surprisingly, I got hired and found out later that he recommended me to the narcotics bureau to work undercover in high school. I was twenty-two but looked like I was about fifteen. After the academy, I was temporarily assigned to the narcotics bureau at a South Bay high school.

Drugs at this school were rampant; it reminded me of my high school. I bought marijuana, hashish, barbiturates, and amphetamines. When you buy drugs, sometimes the dealer will want to you share with him. To feign becoming intoxicated, I would let the dealer light the joint or bong and when passed to me, I would hold my breath while acting as if I were inhaling. Then I would react as the dealer did. If the guy coughed heavily after exhaling, I would do the same. If the guy did nothing, then I did nothing. This must have worked, as a couple of dealers told some students that I rolled the best joints. I have never rolled a joint in my life!

I could see how an officer could easily take some of the drugs he or she confiscated for their own use. Once addicted, patrol officers, officers assigned to the narcotics bureau, or evidence custodians could have a never-ending and free flow of illicit drugs. Sadly, I've known a couple of deputies who became heroin addicts. They were only found out when they would come to the station already in uniform and wearing long-sleeve shirts in the middle of summer to cover their track marks. One guy was in my academy class.

A November 19, 2019, article from the Recovery Village[3], suggests that between 23 and 33 percent of law enforcement officers have alcohol dependency issues. This also includes binge drinking. Per the article, this is twice the national average.

To show the severity of alcohol abuse within law enforcement, the article mentions a study that compared the alcohol use of officers when they first come on the job to their second year and again at the fourth year. None of the officers claimed a drinking problem when they came on the job. At year two, 27 percent claimed alcohol abuse. At year four, 36 percent admitted to abusing alcohol. Going from zero percent to 36 percent over a four-year period is very alarming.

From a personal view, when I joined the LASD, I drank but did not abuse alcohol. I would go running to blow off stress. By my fourth year, and in patrol, I had no time to run. I was on shift work, going to court or working late two or three days a week, and married with two toddlers. I relied more and more on alcohol to relax, either at home or with the fellas a couple times a month. I became part of the 36 percent.

By my ninth year, I had been involved in an on-duty traffic collision where a child died; had been assigned as a detective to location fifty miles from home; had worked a lot of overtime so my wife could stay with the kids and not work outside the home; had a third child, who nearly died from respiratory issues; had gone through a divorce; had lost one brother after he became paralyzed in a traffic accident; had seen the other brother go to prison on a drug and weapons conviction; and had been promoted to a location eighty miles from my home. Alcohol did not help.

The result of these stresses was my becoming like the prodigal son. I had lost sight of relying on the Lord and tried to handle things on my own. However, I never lost my faith, nor did I blame the Lord for any of these trials. My actions were my fault. No one twisted my arm to act as I did. I got back into running and was able to once again handle stress without alcohol.

I mentioned that my youngest child had nearly died as a result of respiratory issues. As she lay in the pediatric intensive care unit (ICU) at nine months, I made a "deal" with God. I told him that if he let me have my little girl, she would be his.

About five years later, she asked me out of the blue, "Daddy, why don't we go to church?" I looked upward and remembered the "deal" that I had made. That Sunday, I went to a church that my partner was attending. About a month later, I accepted Jesus as my Savior in front of the church family.

I received the most awesome and bizarre sensation that I had ever experienced. It felt like the whole room was spinning. Although I saw the people in the church, it felt like there was no one else in the place except me. Everything was in slow motion.

Gradually, awesome things began to happen. I started reading the Bible on a regular basis, I began to tithe, and I was finally able to put the fatal traffic accident behind me that had plagued me for ten years.

It seemed that life got better, but it really didn't. Life was like it had been before, except that I had the one backup who never fails to respond: Jesus. I tended to look a life with a Christian joy, instead of the "my way" or human method of coping.

Suicide

Suicide is the ultimate act of depression. I remember telling my kids that suicide is a permanent solution to a temporary problem. I thank the Lord that my kids took this to heart. They would quote this back to me when telling me of crises that their friends were enduring, which included suicide by overdose.

The Bible contains instances of suicide from depression. These are three examples of people who were placed in positions of authority by God and turned from him. The consequences of their turning from God were dire, to say the least.

Saul

Throughout 1 Samuel, Saul exhibits depression and despair, leading to paranoia that caused him to make several attempts to kill David. Eventually, Saul's despair led to total dysfunction and allowed the Philistines to attack Israel. Not wanting to be killed by the Philistines, Saul fell on his own sword. His suicide caused his armor bearer to fall on his sword as well.

> *The Spirit of the Lord departed from Saul, and sent tor-menting spirit that filled him with depression and fear.*
> —1 Samuel 16:14

Ahithophel

In 2 Samuel, Ahithophel, an adviser of David, defected and served Absalom, David's son. He gave Absalom advice on how to defeat and kill David. Another of David's advisers, Hushai, gave Absalom other advice, which Absalom followed. However, Hushai was still loyal to David and gave the bogus advice to Absalom so David could defeat his son—which is what happened.

Upon hearing that his advice was not heeded and that David knew of the counsel given to Absalom, Ahithophel hanged himself. The Bible does not specifically mention why he hanged himself, but one can surmise that Ahithophel had gone against God's servant, David, becoming full of despair and depression. This is much like Judas Iscariot, who hanged himself after betraying Jesus. Ahithophel, an adviser of David, removed himself from David's service and tried to kill him. Judas, an Apostle of Jesus (a descendant of David) removed himself from Jesus's ministry and turned him over to the Pharisees to be killed.

Zimri

In 1 Kings 16, Zimri, king of Israel, set himself on fire when he learned that the Philistines had captured Tirzah and were coming for him. He was king for only seven days. He did not obey the Lord and became filled with despair and depression.

To me it is not coincidental that these three Old Testament suicides were law enforcement or military related. Throughout the Bible, the Lord has shown his love of law enforcement and military. The Beatitudes give a good description of how we as law enforcement should act (Matthew 5:3–12):

- "Blessed are the poor in spirit, for theirs is the kingdom of heaven." (Relying on God through accepting Jesus)

- "Blessed are those who mourn, for they will be comforted." (Being empathetic to the feelings of others)

- "Blessed are the meek, for they will inherit the earth." (Surrendering to fully God through faith in his Son)

- "Blessed are those who hunger and thirst for righteousness, for they will be filled." (Striving for justice as Jesus directed us)

- "Blessed are the merciful, for they will be shown mercy." (Treating others as we want to be treated for the sake of Christ)

- "Blessed are the pure in heart, for they will see God." (Doing what is right because of your love of God, not just because of man-made policy)

- "Blessed are the peacemakers, for they will be called children of God." (This is why most of us became peace officers.)

- "Blessed are those who are persecuted because of righteousness, for theirs is the kingdom of heaven." Although we are often despised simply because we want to help people, we will gain eternal life if we continue to use these trials to strengthen our faith.

- "Blessed are you when people insult you, persecute you and falsely say all kinds of evil against you because of me. Rejoice and be glad, because great is your reward in heaven, for in the same way they persecuted the prophets who were before you." Don't respond in kind to the insults or verbal barbs thrown at you. Your response should be professional and Christian based. However, in my humble opinion, this does not mean that we should become punching bags or be subject to physical abuse.

Law Enforcement Suicides

The chart below shows the rate of law enforcement on-duty deaths and suicides from 2015 through 2019[4]. On-duty deaths have decreased nearly 17 percent from 165 in 2015 to 134 in 2019. However, suicides increased by 125 percent over the same time period.

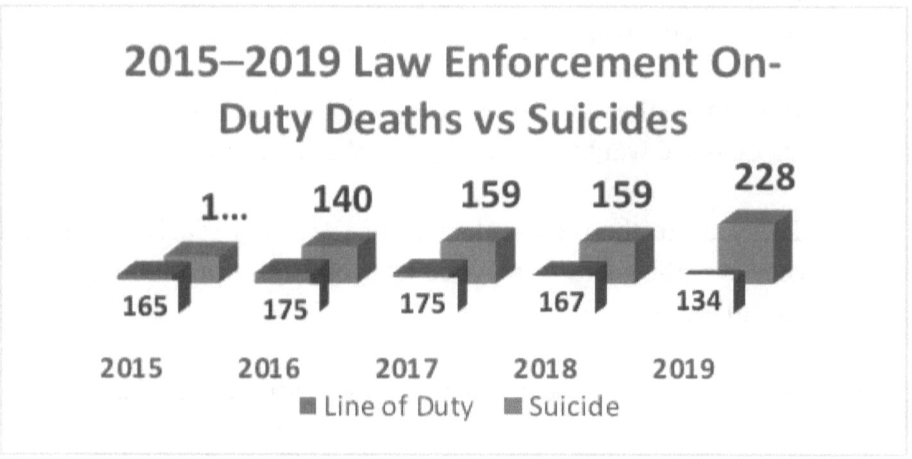

A major factor for this alarming statistic is PTSD from incidents we have witnessed or handled. Per an April 2018 white paper study conducted by the Ruderman Family Foundation[5]:

> A number of factors contributing to mental health issues among first responders and what leads to their elevated rate of suicide. One study included in the white paper found that on average, police officers witness 188 "critical incidents" during their careers. This exposure to trauma can lead to several forms of mental illness. For example, PTSD and depression rates among firefighters and police officers have been found to be as much as 5 times higher than the rates within the civilian population, which causes these first responders to commit suicide at a considerably higher rate. Even when suicide does not occur, untreated mental illness can lead to poor physical health and impaired decision-making.

I believe that another reason for the high suicide rate is the increasing numbers of assaults upon law enforcement. FBI data showed that assaults upon law enforcement from 2015 through 2018 increased by 17 percent, peaking in 2017, which is a 20 percent increase from 2015.[6]

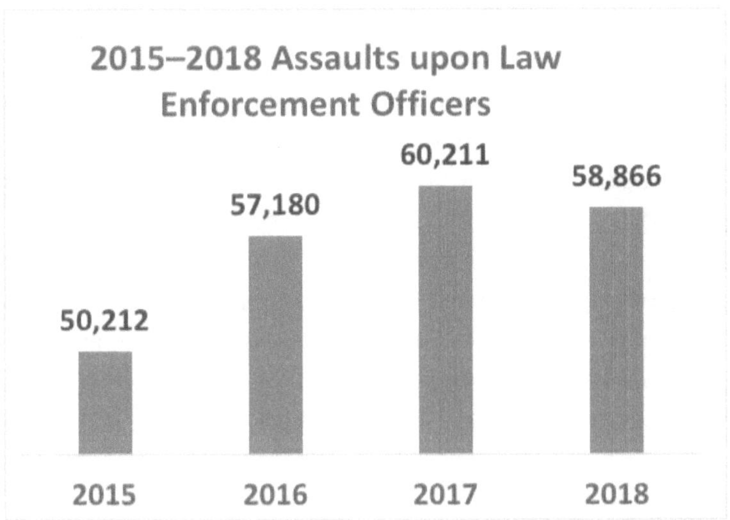

Although the number of officers killed in the line of duty dropped from 2016 to 2019, the number of assaults on law enforcement officers and suicides increased over the same period. I would suggest that there is a correlation between assaults and suicides. It is very difficult to go to work and wonder if you will be injured or will not come home simply because you want to keep the peace and give back to your community. To go through this fear without relying on human coping mechanisms requires true dependence on God. This is only obtained through his Son, Jesus Christ.

And I will do whatever you ask in my name, so that the Father may be glorified in the Son. You may ask me for anything in my name, and I will do it.
—John 14:13–14

I am the way and the truth and the life. No one comes to
the Father except through me.
—John 14:6

There are many reasons for the rise in the assault rate: recent political movements, antipolice groups, media, and video games. Add in relatively new stressful incidents, such as suicide by cop, terrorist attacks, and the increase in active-shooter situations—no wonder the rate of suicides has increased so dramatically in the five-year study. Yet only 3 to 5 percent of law enforcement agencies have suicide-prevention programs.

There are several groups that provide officers immediate counsel in suicide prevention—too many to list here. Go on the internet, and search for "police suicide." Numerous groups in your area will pop up. Keep a list of these groups handy to help your peers or yourself.

War Stories

As a jail deputy, I worked with a guy who committed suicide after learning that his parents had died in a plane crash. Instead of relying on the Lord for strength, his grief consumed him. He shot himself in the head in front of his two toddlers.

As a sergeant, I learned that my former supervising line deputy had committed suicide. He had killed a sergeant seventeen years earlier in the sergeant's vehicle over a woman. The deputy was dating the sergeant's estranged wife and was stalking the woman; he was extremely possessive. The deputy and sergeant had been friends in the past and had worked the same station.

A married male deputy had gotten a female employee pregnant. He became despondent and depressed, killing himself. Now there was a fatherless child and a new widow.

Another deputy whom I worked with committed suicide at the station after he learned that his wife was seeing another man. The wife and the other man, also deputies, eventually married.

In each of these instances, the officers succumbed to earthly stresses. Each one began their careers with enthusiasm, but ended with apathy and depression.

The thought of suicide crossed my mind a few times. However, instead of me hitting rock bottom with a bottle, the Lord came to my rescue, reminding me of my kids, and my walk drastically improved.

If your department, church, or insurance offers counseling services, *use them*. Just make sure that what is suggested follows the Word. In times of personal crisis, it is much better to talk to a professional than one of your buddies at the bar or drinking session after shift.

Retired Officers

Officers who have a relatively healthy balance in their lives look forward to retirement. These officers have their retirement activities planned out. Some will work another job in a field they like; others will travel. Several will spend their golden years with grandkids, and quite a few are volunteers in their churches or nonprofit groups.

When talking with my peers, I learned that many do not plan for life after law enforcement. We don't accept change very well. We tend to enjoy a comfortable routine that we have control over. I am amazed when I see officers with over forty years of service or who are over sixty-five and still working. Retirement to some represents losing control of their life. Some fear the unknown. Other can't give up the high social status and authority associated with law enforcement. They remind me of Pharisees with phylacteries and tassels.

The experts in the law and the Pharisees sit on Moses' seat. Therefore, pay attention to what they tell you and do it. But do not do what they do, for they do not practice what they teach. They tie up heavy loads, hard to carry, and put them on men's shoulders, but they themselves are not willing even to lift a finger to move them.

*They do all their deeds to be seen by people, for they
make their phylacteries wide and their tassels long.*
—Matthew 23:2–5

*They pour out their arrogant words; all the evildoers
boast.*
—Psalms 94:4

*For by the grace given to me I say to everyone among
you not to think of himself more highly than he ought to
think, but to think with sober judgment, each according
to the measure of faith that God has assigned.*
—Romans 12:3

Some deputies have told me that they don't know if they can handle their spouse twenty-four seven. This requires an adjustment. On my Facebook page I wrote, "I've been blessed that I have a great wife and that she still likes to be around me after I retired!" This is not only true for the retired officer, but the spouse as well. It's not easy for the officer's spouse having them around all the time.

Some officers simply do not want to be at home. They may have marital issues, don't want to be a babysitter for grandkids or aging parents, or simply don't want to handle domestic or home-related issues.

Some officers have to cede a portion of their pension to an ex-spouse. It's tough enough to give a piece of your pension to an ex-spouse if you are alone, but the issue becomes intensified when the officer remarries. This creates double grief. Being forced to give a portion of your pension to someone not in your life and then catching all types of endless grief from the current spouse each time the pension check comes in is too much for some to handle. Too many of my partners have entered retirement this way.

I had a plan upon retirement, but my plans fell through. I went from working a minimum of forty hours a week to zero in one day. It sounds like an easy transition, but it is not. I got my real estate license to work with my wife, but I do not have the patience of a saint that my wife has and that is required to be successful. I got a substitute teaching credential for elementary and middle school. After I nearly got fired and called into the principal's office for telling an exceptionally unruly class to "shut up," I decided this was not for me. I never got called into the principal's office, even when I was in school, and then I get called in at the age of sixty. Teachers are true heroes!

I was pretty depressed sitting home with virtually nothing to do. Only after I became actively involved in my church was I able to accept retirement.

This verse had been ringing in my ears for years: "Today, if you will hear His voice, do not harden your hearts" (Heb. 3:15).

But I was afraid and anxious to take the step and listen to the Lord. I was afraid that I would fail the Lord. After thirty-two years of working the streets and jails of Los Angeles County, I was afraid to work for God. I'm glad I took the leap of faith. Again, life seemed to improve. What really improved was my walk with the Lord. I now look forward to sharing my faith instead of worrying that my friends may be offended.

> *For whoever is ashamed of me and of my words, of him*
> *will the Son of Man be ashamed when he comes in his*
> *glory and the glory of the Father and of the holy angels.*
> —Luke 9:26

Retirement is a well-earned reward for years of public service. This is a reason why some plan is needed in advance of retirement. If you fail to plan, you plan to fail! However, remember: "And whatever you do, in word or deed, do everything in the name of the Lord Jesus, giving thanks to God the Father through him" (Col. 3:17).

Suicide among retired or separated law enforcement officers is also an issue. While the rates are not as high as active officers, they are still significant. A report by the *International Journal of Emergency Mental Health*[7] provided data from a fifty-year study regarding suicide rates of active and retired law enforcement officers. The data presented showed that officers in their last five years have the highest rate of suicide. The study suggests that the anxiety associated with the impending retirement and failure to plan for lifestyle change are responsible. In my department, we are advised to meet with our retirement association when we have five years left to work. Many do, and many don't.

I worked with two deputies who committed suicide after retirement because they couldn't handle their home lives.

War Stories

In one instance, he and his wife constantly bickered. In the middle of an argument, he said that he was done and walked into the bedroom. His wife thought he had enough arguing. But within seconds of him entering the bedroom, she heard a single gunshot. He had taken his life. There was no emotional outburst, note, history of prior suicide attempts, or sign of suicidal ideation.

The other deputy I worked with for over twelve years. He was a good street cop, training officer, dispatcher, and watch deputy. After he retired, he fell victim to not wanting to be at home, as he and his wife didn't get along very well. He started drinking again, which brought up an old stomach ailment.

He told his wife, also a retired deputy, that he couldn't live with the stomach issues and talked about suicide. His wife took all his guns, she thought. He had hidden one pistol—the one he took his life with.

Resist Satan

We cannot let Satan get into our head and make us weary or tired of following the Word. We must stand tall and remain steadfast in the Lord. A few years of being persecuted on earth for the sake of Jesus is more than worth our reward. In addition, God has promised that he will never forsake us or give us more than we can bear. Remember that freedom is never free. Jesus paid the ultimate price for our freedom, yet we are asked so little in return for the freedom that he provided. If we can look at eternal life in this way, staying on the straight and narrow is easier.

> *Put on all of God's armor so that you will be able to stand firm against all strategies of the devil. For we are not fighting against flesh-and-blood enemies, but against evil rulers and authorities of the unseen world, against mighty powers in this dark world, and against evil spirits in the heavenly places.*
>
> *Therefore, put on every piece of God's armor so you will be able to resist the enemy in the time of evil. Then after the battle you will still be standing firm. Stand your ground, putting on the belt of truth and the body armor of God's righteousness. For shoes, put on the peace that comes from the Good News so that you will be fully prepared. In addition to all of these, hold up the shield of faith to stop the fiery arrows of the devil. Put on salvation as your helmet, and take the sword of the Spirit, which is the word of God. Pray in the Spirit at all times and on every occasion. Stay alert and be persistent in your prayers for all believers everywhere.*
> —Ephesians 6:11–18

We need to remain strong in our faith and not give up. We've all felt like throwing in the towel and taking the easy way out to meet our human needs. But God provides strength to defeat apathy through the Word and the examples of Jesus, the apostles, and the prophets. It's not always easy, but it can be done through God.

> *As for the rest of you, dear brothers and sisters, never get tired of doing good. Take note of those who refuse to obey what we say in this letter. Stay away from them so*

*they will be ashamed. Don't think of them as enemies,
but warn them as you would a brother or sister.*
—2 Thessalonians 3:13–15

*Oh, the joys of those who do not follow the advice of the
wicked, or stand around with sinners, or join in with
mockers. But they delight in the law of the Lord, medi-
tating on it day and night.*

*They are like trees planted along the riverbank, bearing
fruit each season. Their leaves never wither, and they
prosper in all they do. But not the wicked! They are
like worthless chaff, scattered by the wind. They will be
condemned at the time of judgment. Sinners will have
no place among the godly. For the Lord watches over
the path of the godly, but the path of the wicked leads to
destruction.*
—Psalms 1:1–6

We enter our careers with enthusiasm and usually leave them beaten up. We can end our careers with enthusiasm if we believe. In Haggai, Zerubbabel fervently started to rebuild God's temple. However, the building stopped when the neighboring Samaritans opposed the temple. Instead of rebuilding the temple, the people built themselves beautiful houses and vineyards, neglecting the Lord. The results were a drought and poor harvest (eat and not satisfied; drink and still be thirsty), loss of revenue (holes in your pockets), and diminished living standards (clothes will not keep you warm).

When Zerubbabel was reinvigorated and finished the temple, the Lord said, "So, the Lord sparked the enthusiasm of Zerubbabel son of Shealtiel, governor of Judah, and the enthusiasm of Jeshua son of Jehozadak, the high priest, and the enthusiasm of the whole remnant of God's people. They began to work on the house of their God, the Lord of Heaven's Armies" (Hag. 1:14).

But when this happens, says the Lord of Heaven's Armies, I will honor you, Zerubbabel son of Shealtiel, my servant. I will make you like a signet ring on my finger, says the LORD, for I have chosen you. I, the LORD of Heaven's Armies, have spoken!
—Haggai 2:18

The future glory of this Temple will be greater than its past glory, says the Lord of Heaven's Armies. And in this place, I will bring peace. I, the Lord of Heaven's Armies, have spoken!
—Haggai 2:9

The Lord commended Zerubbabel for removing his apathy and re-committing himself to the Lord. In reality, the rebuilt temple was used to prophesize the coming of Jesus. Like Zerubbabel, we are also blessed by the Lord when we do not fall into apathy and we follow his word—although we do not deserve it. We will be right with the Lord, or as my brother-in-law used to say, "It's all Kool & the Gang."

CHAPTER 5

Perseverance and Patience

Let perseverance finish its work so that you may be mature and complete.
—James 1:4

Blessed is the one who perseveres under trial because, having stood the test, that person will receive the crown of life that the Lord has promised to those who love him.
—James 1:12

Be patient, then, brothers and sisters, until the Lord's coming. See how the farmer waits for the land to yield its valuable crop, patiently waiting for the autumn and spring rains. You too, be patient and stand firm, because the Lord's coming is near. Don't grumble against one another, brothers and sisters, or you will be judged. The Judge is standing at the door!
—James 5:7

A nineteenth-century British missionary in China, Hudson Taylor, said, "There are three indispensable requirements for a missionary: 1. Patience 2. Patience 3. Patience."

Our mission is to serve our community in a way that Christ directs us. This requires great patience and perseverance.

Perseverance requires faith and is trait that law enforcement officers must have. We have hope or a belief that we will be successful and have a long career. If we do not have faith, then we have no hope. If we have no hope, then why go through the difficulties and heartaches associated with reaching our goal as a Christian law enforcement officer?

> *For in this hope we were saved. But hope that is seen is no hope at all. Who hopes for what they already have? But if we hope for what we do not yet have, we wait for it patiently.*
> —Romans 8:24–25

> *Because you have kept the word of My perseverance, I also will keep you from the hour of testing, that hour which is about to come upon the whole world, to test those who dwell on the earth.*
> —Revelation 3:10

> *Here is the perseverance of the saints who keep the commandments of God and their faith in Jesus.*
> —Revelation 14:12

> *And in your knowledge, self-control, and in your self-control, perseverance, and in your perseverance, godliness.*
> —2 Peter 1:6

*And you have perseverance and have endured for My
name's sake, and have not grown weary.*
—Revelation 2:3

*So that you won't become lazy but will be imitators of
those who inherit the promises through faith and perseverance…*
—Hebrews 6:12

*And he believed the Lord, and he counted it to him as
righteousness.*
—Genesis 15:6

*It was not through the law that Abraham and his off-
spring received the promise that he would be heir of
the world, but through the righteousness that comes by
faith.*
—Romans 4:13

Paul tells Timothy of the prize gained by faith and perseverance:

I have fought the good fight, I have finished the race,
and I have remained faithful. And now the prize awaits
me—the crown of righteousness, which the Lord, the
righteous Judge, will give me on the day of his return.
And the prize is not just for me but for all who eagerly
look forward to his appearing. (2 Tim. 4:7–8)

Law enforcement is one of the few professions that require faith on
a minute-by-minute basis. We have no idea what types of situations we
will handle or whether we will go home at the end of our shift. Also,
without faith, we cannot be saved or go home to Jesus. Jesus stated that
without God, man cannot be saved; it is impossible: "The disciples were
astounded. 'Then who in the world can be saved?' they asked. Jesus looked

at them intently and said, 'Humanly speaking, it is impossible. But with God everything is possible'" (Matt. 19:25–26).

The Bible lists several examples of perseverance to inspire us:

- Paul: The former persecutor of Christians who became the apostle to the Gentiles.

- I have worked much harder, been in prison more frequently, been flogged more severely, and been exposed to death again and again. Five times I received from the Jews the forty lashes minus one. Three times I was beaten with rods, once I was pelted with stones, three times I was shipwrecked, I spent a night and a day in the open sea, I have been constantly on the move. I have been in danger from rivers, in danger from bandits, in danger from my fellow Jews, in danger from Gentiles; in danger in the city, in danger in the country, in danger at sea; and in danger from false believers. I have labored and toiled and have often gone without sleep; I have known hunger and thirst and have often gone without food; I have been cold and naked. Besides everything else, I face daily the pressure of my concern for all the churches. (2 Cor. 11:22–33)

- The man healed at the pool of Bethesda: In John 5:1–18, Jesus heals a man who had been an invalid for thirty-eight years, yet still believed that the Lord could heal him by entering into the pool ahead of everyone else. Jesus saw him and asked if he wanted to be healed, to which the man said, *"Yes!"* Jesus told the man to pick up his mat and go. The man was instantly healed.

- Bleeding woman: In Luke 43:43–48, Jesus heals a woman who had been bleeding for twelve years. She had spent every penny she had relying on doctors and modern medicine of the time to heal her. She persevered in her quest by merely touching Jesus's clothing. She was instantly completely healed by the only way possible: faith in Jesus.

- The parable of the man who asked for bread: This is a story of a man who at midnight asked his friend for some bread. His friend tells him no, that it is too late. The man continues to ask for bread. Eventually, the friend gives the man bread: "But I tell you this—though he won't do it for friendship's sake, if you keep knocking long enough, he will get up and give you whatever you need because of your shameless persistence. So, I say to you: Ask and it will be given to you; seek and you will find; knock and the door will be opened to you" (Luke 11:8–9).

- The Samaritan woman: In John 4, Jesus is speaking to a Samaritan woman. This in itself is noteworthy, as Jews and Samaritans did not associate with each other, and as he was speaking to a woman. This account teaches three lessons. It shows what faith can do, it shows that you should love your neighbor, and it shows that Jesus is the Savior for all—not just the Jews.

  "I know that Messiah" (called Christ) "is coming.
  When he comes, he will explain everything to us." Then
  Jesus declared, "I, the one speaking to you—I am he."
  —John 4:25–26.

Of all the accounts of perseverance in the Bible, the story of Job is probably best known. God was boasting of Job's faith and was met by Satan. Satan said that the only reason Job was so obedient was that he was wealthy. God disagreed and allowed Satan to put Job through three trials.

1. Job's livestock, servants, and ten children died or were killed (upset).

2. He became afflicted with many sores, with his wife berating him. She told him to give up, kill himself, and curse the Lord for his afflictions (depressed).

3. His three friends gave their advice (based upon human knowledge) as to why Job had been struck with so much calamity. They reason that Job must have sinned greatly against God, breaking the law (angry).

Job was understandably upset, depressed, and angry. However, his response was not to turn away from God, but to seek him. God saw that Job passed his trials with flying colors. He spoke with Job and explained that human knowledge (the advice of his three friends) was worthless and that believers do not always understand how the Lord works in their lives. Job acknowledged this and was blessed by the Lord with twice as much as before the trials.

I'll share a Joblike story that I witnessed in my life. My partner, who took me to the church where I was saved, lost his job. The allegations were totally bogus, having been brought up by his ex-wife. I know this because I saw the so-called "evidence" presented, and I spoke to an IA investigator. None of the executives who reviewed the investigation had the integrity to question the merit or facts of the charge. The executives were told by their supervisor to let him fight to get his job back. My buddy never got his job back and went over a year without a regular job. He went through all his saved leave time, deferred compensation, and personal savings. He also had his adult daughter and two grandkids living with him.

Instead of becoming bitter or drowning his sorrows in a bottle, he strengthened his walk. He regularly attended church, becoming part of the pastor's security team that went to the Holy Land. My buddy was understandably upset, but he never lost or questioned his faith. As for the executive who said to let him fight to get his job back, that man ended up in a federal prison for conspiracy. I am very proud of the victory over a huge trial that my buddy won through his faith in Jesus Christ.

Definition and Example

Wikipedia describes *patience* thus: "Patience (or forbearance) is the ability to endure difficult circumstances such as perseverance in the face of delay; tolerance of provocation without responding in annoyance/anger; or forbearance when under strain, especially when faced with longer-term difficulties. Patience is the level of endurance one can have before negativity."

The *Merriam-Webster Dictionary* describes *perseverance* as: "continued effort to do or achieve something despite difficulties, failure, or opposition : the action or condition or an instance of persevering : STEADFASTNESS."

To illustrate the need for perseverance in our law enforcement career, I'll use the Los Angeles County Sheriff's Department hiring process as an example.

Those who worship the Lord on a special day do it to honor him. Those who eat any kind of food do so to honor the Lord, since they give thanks to God before eating. And those who refuse to eat certain foods also want to please the Lord and give thanks to God. For we don't live for ourselves or die for ourselves. If we live, it's to honor the Lord. And if we die, it's to honor the Lord. So, whether we live or die, we belong to the Lord.

1. Application / supplemental questions
Job requirements, work conditions, and prebackground questionnaire.

2. Written test vocabulary

Reading comprehension: Tests your ability to read and understand what is being communicated in short and medium-size passages.

Writing—clarity: Tests your ability to write with clarity and conciseness.

Writing—spelling: Tests your ability to spell commonly misspelled words.

Writing—grammar: Tests grammar usage.

Deductive reasoning: Tests your ability to reason deductively or to conclude a specific or particular point from a general principle.

Inductive reasoning: Tests your ability to reason inductively or to conclude a large principle from specific or particular points.

Data interpretation: Tests your ability to work with records and numbers.

3. Validated Physical Ability Test (VPAT): Two opportunities in six months to pass

Push-up test: Determines strength of the applicant.

Seventy-five-yard run: Simulating a foot pursuit, the run requires the applicant to run seventy-five yards, make several turns during the run, and jump over several curblike obstacles.

Sit-up test: Evaluates abdominal strength.

Twenty-meter shuttle run: Assesses cardiovascular endurance and involves running a series of laps between two lines twenty meters apart.

4. Oral Interview / Intake

A formal interview to determine job interest and communication skills. Complete live scan fingerprints.

5. Complete and submit a Web Personal History Statement (WEBPHS) online and upload notarized waiver.

6. Background investigation

An investigator will conduct an extensive review of the applicant's personal history, financial records, and interviews of neighbors. As part of this phase, a polygraph test will be given, and the applicant is required to complete a ride-along at a patrol station and to tour one of the jail facilities.

7. Admin review

Once the background is completed, the applicant's file will be submitted for an administrative review.

8. Psychological evaluation

A four-hour written test and interview with a departmental psychologist.

9. Medical examination

10. Pre-academy consultation

Meet with the captain of the personnel administration bureau.

The entire preemployment process takes, on average, between six and nine months to complete. Only if you pass all ten of these preemployment items are you assigned to the academy, which is between twenty and twenty-six weeks long.

For 2019, LASD showed the following data[8]:

- 20,857 Deputy Sheriff Trainee applications were received

- 1,087 or 5.2% of these applicants were hired

- 695 or 64% of the applicants that were hired graduated the academy

- Only 3.3% of all applicants graduated the academy

The applicant failure rate for LASD and departments throughout California is very high. In a July 25, 2019, report, the California Commission on Peace Officers Standards and Training (POST)[9], estimated that between 90 and 95 percent of all applicants do not pass their department's preemployment process. The primary issues causing the high applicant failure were weak academic performance (primarily in reading and writing), weak fitness levels, and deficits in character and behavior. This means that out of one thousand applicants, only fifty to one hundred people make it to the academy. (POST is the governmental entity that creates and maintains peace officer standards and training throughout California.)

Academy

After passing all the pre-academy requirements, you enter the academy. The academy has its own perseverance issues. POST mandates that all peace officers must complete required courses. There are forty-two mandated courses or domains that an applicant must complete before becoming a peace officer in California. These domains range from law to community relations to weapons training to physical fitness. These domains are designed to be as diverse as the tasks we handle on a daily basis. Applicants are given several opportunities to pass the mandated domains; however, the applicant will be terminated if not all are completed.

In addition to the POST-mandated domains, the drill instructors yell and "get in the face" of applicants to simulate the harassment (persecution) that officers will be subject to when working with the public. Some people can't handle this aspect of training and either quit or verbally "go off" on the drill instructors. If this behavior continues, the applicant is terminated for their inability to handle stress.

Some academies require that the applicant live on campus for the duration of the academy and away from the daily support of friends and family. This adds another layer of stress and perseverance into the mix.

The curricula for police academies has changed over the years since I went through in 1982. "Old heads" will complain that new academy graduates had it easy. New graduates will complain how tough the academy was. It doesn't matter; the academy is a stressful period of many trials that will test and refine your perseverance.

First Assignment / Training

After academy graduation the new officer receives his or her first assignment. In most cases, this will be the first time that the officer will be in a hands-on environment with no instructors or monitors. It will be very obvious that you are new and unexperienced. Be prepared to accept that many people will take advantage of you. It happened to me both in the jails and on the streets. Although the new officer goes through a structured training or probationary period with a training officer, most lessons learned are by trial and error.

In addition to learning a new profession while dealing with society at their worst, up close and personal, many veteran officers or old guys (OGs) feel that it is their duty to give new officers a hard time until they get off probation or complete training. I know that this is considered hazing.

I looked up "hazing" in a thesaurus and found the following synonyms: baptism of fire, martyrdom, initiation, rite of passage. Some forms of hazing are unnecessary and detrimental to the development of a new officer. I definitely am not advocating this type of behavior. Yet, as law enforcement is a quasi-military profession, there are times when you must just suck it up. The basis for this behavior among peers is to develop a thick skin so you can deflect verbal barbs launched against you by the public. Also, this builds camaraderie and trust between you and your peers. At times, this trust includes putting your life in the hands of your peers, which is unique to any other profession, except the military and firefighting.

I was subject to some of these rites of passages, and I didn't like it. However, it never got to the point where it impeded my growth as a deputy sheriff. Actually, I had to keep from laughing at times, as I knew this was part of training and did not take their actions seriously. This was a strategy that I also used in the academy when drill instructors would get in my face. Drill instructors would truly get angry when I would fight to keep a straight face when being yelled at. I was blessed. My dad spent four years in the army during the Korean War, and he instilled in my siblings and myself responsibility, discipline, and integrity. He did this through his actions more than his words. We learned via observing his character. Also, he taught me how to spit-shine shoes by the age of ten.

> *People who accept discipline are on the pathway to life,*
> *but those who ignore correction will go astray.*
> —Proverbs 10:17

> *To learn, you must love discipline; it is stupid to hate*
> *correction.*
> —Proverbs 12:1

When my training was over, I was instantly accepted and trusted by the "old heads." This did not mean that I conducted business as they did, as I did not want to become "one of the boys." I did not always agree with how they conducted business. Nevertheless, a bond of trust was created.

However, when I saw them behave badly or act inappropriately, I let them know, whether I was their peer or supervisor.

When I became a training officer, I treated my trainees in a very firm and fair manner. Once my trainee learned the basics of being a patrol officer, then I would let him or her make decisions on their own, with me taking a back seat. This is much like watching your child take their first steps. You sit back and smile about how much they have learned.

I must acknowledge my training officer, John Harris, who taught me the right way of being a deputy sheriff by his actions. He showed me to treat everyone with respect, not to take myself too seriously, and to turn in complete reports that made it easier for detectives to get criminal filings.

I was extremely fortunate that he was assigned to me. As I look back at it now, the Lord was watching over me in the situation that he had placed me in by assigning John as my training officer. I passed on the lessons learned from John to the deputies that I trained, supervised, or managed over my career.

Salvation and eternal life are our goals and gained via godly perseverance. To put this in a law enforcement perspective, we spend our careers assisting others. If we persevere, we gain a lifetime pension as an earned reward. As Christians, we should spend our lives (careers) helping others as Jesus directs us. If we persevere, we gain eternal life as a reward. If you notice, I did not say *earned* reward. We cannot "earn" eternal life. Eternal life is the gift of grace from God through Jesus.

> *Eternal life is not a gift from God: eternal life is the gift of God.*
> —Oswald Chambers

Listening and Doing

> *Understand this, my dear brothers and sisters: You must all be quick to listen, slow to speak, and slow to get angry. Human anger does not produce the righteousness*

God desires. So, get rid of all the filth and evil in your lives, and humbly accept the word God has planted in your hearts, for it has the power to save your souls.

But don't just listen to God's word. You must do what it says. Otherwise, you are only fooling yourselves. For if you listen to the word and don't obey, it is like glancing at your face in a mirror. You see yourself, walk away, and forget what you look like. But if you look carefully into the perfect law that sets you free, and if you do what it says and don't forget what you heard, then God will bless you for doing it.
—James 1:19–25

We hear the Word, yet we often don't do what it says. It isn't easy. Without constant reinforcement to do what is right, we tend to fall back on our human habits. This is why law enforcement has constant training and policy manuals. Our departments want to reinforce in us what is necessary to complete our daily tasks professionally and ethically. We don't always like what our departments tell us. However, if we want to continue in our chosen profession, we accept this discipline and do it—except what is contrary to the Bible.

Without the constant reinforcement from the Bible, we cannot complete our daily tasks in the manner dictated by God and exemplified by Jesus. We don't always like what we have to do, but we accept God's way and do it. If not, we lose a lot more than our temporary earthly job in law enforcement.

No discipline is enjoyable while it is happening—it's painful! But afterward there will be a peaceful harvest of right living for those who are trained in this way.
—Hebrews 12:11

James says listening to the word and not obeying it is like "like glancing at your face in a mirror. You see yourself, walk away, and forget what you look like." It goes hand in hand with the parable of the seed and soil:

> Listen! A farmer went out to plant some seeds. As he scattered them across his field, some seeds fell on a footpath, and the birds came and ate them. Other seeds fell on shallow soil with underlying rock. The seeds sprouted quickly because the soil was shallow. But the plants soon wilted under the hot sun, and since they didn't have deep roots, they died. Other seeds fell among thorns that grew up and choked out the tender plants. Still other seeds fell on fertile soil, and they produced a crop that was thirty, sixty, and even a hundred times as much as had been planted! Anyone with ears to hear should listen and understand. His disciples came and asked him, "Why do you use parables when you talk to the people?" He replied, "You are permitted to understand the secrets of the Kingdom of Heaven, but others are not." (Matt. 13:3–9)

Seeds that were eaten by birds before sprouting or seeds that wilted in the sun are those that forget what they look like when they walk away from the mirror. Some people listen to what others say and don't give themselves the opportunity to hear the Word (birds eating the seeds). Others hear the Word but shirk when they need to act (shallow soil). Still others, after hearing the Word, fall back into their human ways (fell among thorns and were choked out).

Seeds that fell on fertile soil and produced great crops are the ones that do not forget what they look like in the mirror. They look carefully and see the one who sets us free (Jesus). If we truly believe, we are blessed by God for doing what Jesus says.

War Stories

I was in briefing, and a new station order came out mandating some type of extra documentation. I remember most of veteran OG deputies whined and complained. I told them that I didn't like the new mandate, either, as I had to track the new documentation. But as the documentation was neither illegal nor unethical, we needed to do as directed. I said it was their choice as to whether they complied or not.

The choice to comply was the deputies, not mine. Failure to comply may have resulted in some minor type written documentation (discipline/punishment).

Jesus often delivered unpopular messages. In John 6, Jesus teaches that he is the Bread of Life. John states that the people began to argue and become agitated as he claimed to have come down from heaven. Jesus told them to quit complaining. To be saved, we must eat his body and drink his blood. His disciples began to complain that this teaching was too difficult.

Jesus explained that the teaching was about eternal life (not cannibalism) and that human effort does nothing. After the explanation, many disciples left him. It was their choice to stay or go. He did not beg them to stay. Instead he asked the apostles if they were leaving also. To this, Peter replied to whom would they follow. The apostles believed and knew that Jesus was the Messiah.

The deputies and the disciples who left Jesus were given the option to choose what they wanted to do after hearing an unpopular mandate.

> *Jesus replied, "But even more blessed are all who hear the word of God and put it into practice."*
> —Luke 11:28

Training

Throughout this chapter, the need for training to overcome our trials and remain steadfast in our faith in Jesus has been discussed. This training comes in the form of wanting to please God while serving others. If we rely solely on our human intuition and knowledge, we may be successful in one situation but fail in the next. We may win the battle but lose the war when we do things for our own need or glory.

We go through the same thing in law enforcement. We are often persecuted for simply doing our jobs. Through the academy and in-service training, we are taught self-discipline and how to handle situations when we are berated. Our training hones or refines our natural inclination to respond in kind to how we are treated. Our training is discipline, not punishment.

Paul and Job are great examples of going through trials. Through their trials, God refined their faith and showed the reward that will come to each of us if we truly believe and live as God wants us to. The testing or refining came in the form of discipline—not punishment. Job was not punished, as he did nothing wrong. God allowed Satan to test him. He lost everything and was also given painful sores. His friends accused him of being evil and said his sons were responsible for their own deaths. Job did not forsake God. In fact, he knew his witness was in heaven, an advocate and a mediator (Jesus): "Even now my witness is in heaven. My advocate is there on high. My friends scorn me, but I pour out my tears to God. I need someone to mediate between God and me, as a person mediates between friends" (Job 16:19–21).

Paul was persecuted numerous times. Like Job, Paul was also tormented by Satan and also passed his test. He reveled in being thought worthy to suffer for Christ. Although Paul was obedient to Christ and went to Rome as directed, he continued to be tested and disciplined:

> So, to keep me from becoming proud, I was given a
> thorn in my flesh, a messenger from Satan to torment
> me and keep me from becoming proud. Three different
> times I begged the Lord to take it away. Each time he
> said, "My grace is all you need. My power works best in
> weakness." So now I am glad to boast about my weak-
> nesses, so that the power of Christ can work through
> me. That's why I take pleasure in my weaknesses, and

in the insults, hardships, persecutions, and troubles
that I suffer for Christ. For when I am weak, then I am
strong. (2 Cor. 12:7–10)

As a runner, this verse made sense to me and allowed me to understand testing and self-discipline. I used to read this verse just before races when I ran track and cross country in high school, college, the Police Olympics, and the Baker-to-Vegas Relay. It got me in the right frame of mind and cleared my head so I was ready to go when the race started. Now I see the verse as a reminder of God continuing to refine and mold me, through Jesus, into what he wants me to be.

A pastor at my church gave an excellent example of discipline via trials in a recent sermon. As a parent, he denied his children dessert for a while. He told them that he was not punishing them but teaching them that they cannot have what they want all the time. He was teaching them self-discipline. His kids questioned him and said that they didn't like the discipline, but they obeyed him out of love and respect. This is exactly what God does for us, and how he wants us to react.

*So be truly glad. There is wonderful joy ahead, even
though you must endure many trials for a little while.
These trials will show that your faith is genuine. It is
being tested as fire tests and purifies gold—though
your faith is far more precious than mere gold. So,
when your faith remains strong through many trials, it
will bring you much praise and glory and honor on the
day when Jesus Christ is revealed to the whole world.
You love him even though you have never seen him.
Though you do not see him now, you trust him; and you
rejoice with a glorious, inexpressible joy. The reward
for trusting him will be the salvation of your souls.*
—1 Peter 1:6–9

*Of course, you get no credit for being patient if you are
beaten for doing wrong. But if you suffer for doing good
and endure it patiently, God is pleased with you. For
God called you to do good, even if it means suffering,
just as Christ suffered for you. He is your example, and
you must follow in his steps.*
—1 Peter 2:20–21

However, if we rely solely on God, then we will be successful in all
things. We will win the war against evil and receive the gift of eternal
life—if we live our lives as God wants us to. This can only occur when
we live our lives as Jesus exemplified through his teachings and actions.

Remember, Satan is the leader of the band of angels that defied God.
He copies God in all he does. God has the Trinity: the Father, Son, and
Holy Spirit. Satan has one also: himself, the beast, and the false prophet.
God's servants will have the seal placed upon them (Rev. 7:3). Satan's
followers will have the mark of the beast (Rev. 13:16). Isaiah 14 describes
Satan's wish to be above God and ultimate demise:

How you are fallen from heaven, O shining star, son of
the morning! You have been thrown down to the earth,
you who destroyed the nations of the world. For you
said to yourself, "I will ascend to heaven and set my
throne above God's stars. I will preside on the mountain
of the gods far away in the north. I will climb to the
highest heavens and be like the Most High." Instead,
you will be brought down to the place of the dead, down
to its lowest depths. (Isa. 14:12–15)

Satan's mutiny is documented throughout the Bible, from Genesis to
Revelation. He uses a chain of command and expects orders to be carried out. For this reason, I believe that law enforcement, military, and
fire are more susceptible to his attacks. We are allowed to go through

more crisis-ridden incidents and integrity-testing situations than most other professions.

> *Stay alert! Watch out for your great enemy, the devil. He prowls around like a roaring lion, looking for someone to devour. Stand firm against him, and be strong in your faith. Remember that your family of believers all over the world is going through the same kind of suffering you are.*
> —1 Peter 5:8–9

> *Beware of false prophets who come disguised as harmless sheep but are really vicious wolves. You can identify them by their fruit, that is, by the way they act. Can you pick grapes from thorn bushes, or figs from thistles? A good tree produces good fruit, and a bad tree produces bad fruit. A good tree can't produce bad fruit, and a bad tree can't produce good fruit. So, every tree that does not produce good fruit is chopped down and thrown into the fire. Yes, just as you can identify a tree by its fruit, so you can identify people by their actions.*
> —Matthew 7:15–20

This is why reading Bible daily is so important. We review departmental procedures regularly to ensure that we act within policy. We should use scripture in the same vein—to ensure that we act as Christians and keep us close to God. This will greatly help us walk the "straight and narrow": "But the gateway to life is very narrow and the road is difficult, and only a few ever find it" (Matt. 7:14).

The way you train is the way you react. Training allows us to act instinctively so we can control our response and emotions. Reading the Word and being faithful to what it says provides us the confidence and godly knowledge to handle any situation. Sometimes, we have the luxury of time to think about our actions, citing Bible verses as a reference. Other times, we make the split-second decision, confident that the Holy Spirit will guide our actions in immediate situations. If you fail to plan, then plan to fail. Jesus is our only plan. If we don't have him, we fail.

CHAPTER 6

Wisdom

*If any of you lacks wisdom, you should ask God, who
gives generously to all without finding fault, and it will
be given to you. But when you ask, you must believe
and not doubt, because the one who doubts is like a
wave of the sea, blown and tossed by the wind. That
person should not expect to receive anything from the
Lord. Such a person is double-minded and unstable in
all they do.*

—James 1:5–8

Wisdom is knowledge, learning, judgment, and understanding. It does
not include perfection. Although none of us are worthy, this means that
we can attain wisdom and other gifts if we use sound biblical judgment
and have a basic understanding of the knowledge of God. I used a basic
knowledge, as no one has a complete understanding of God. We know
what he wants, but often not why.

*For the Lord grants wisdom! From his mouth come
knowledge and understanding. He grants a treasure of*

common sense to the honest. He is a shield to those who walk with integrity.
—Proverbs 4:6–7

Oh, how great are God's riches and wisdom and knowledge! How impossible it is for us to understand his decisions and his ways! For who can know the Lord 's thoughts? Who knows enough to give him advice?
—Romans 11:33–34

We aren't going to achieve 100 percent perfection, nor will we pass each trial that comes up in our lives. We are imperfect humans who make mistakes and continually fight our natural sinful inclinations. However, we persevere and do not give up. If we continue in our faith in Jesus and continue to live by his example, we can obtain one of the most precious gifts that God can give us: wisdom.

Don't be deceived, my dear brothers and sisters. Every good and perfect gift is from above, coming down from the Father of the heavenly lights, who does not change like shifting shadows. He chose to give us birth through the word of truth, that we might be a kind of first fruits of all he created.
—James 1:16–18

Wisdom is so important that there are several books in the Bible that deal with this gift as the main theme: the books of Proverbs, Psalms, Job, and Ecclesiastes, and Song of Solomon. Additionally, Jesus made several references to these books throughout the New Testament. God's favor and Jesus's wisdom increased hand in hand.

There the child grew up healthy and strong. He was filled with wisdom, and God's favor was on him.
—Luke 2:40

Jesus grew in wisdom and in stature and in favor with God and all the people.
—Luke 2:52

Definition of Wisdom

The *Merriam-Webster Dictionary* defines *wisdom* as:

> 1a: ability to discern inner qualities and relationships : INSIGHT

> b: good sense: JUDGMENT

> c: generally accepted belief challenges what has become accepted wisdom among many historians—Robert Darnton

> d: accumulated philosophical or scientific learning: KNOWLEDGE

> 2: a wise attitude, belief, or course of action

> 3: the teachings of the ancient wise men

The Bible describes wisdom as seven pillars. They have been described in different terms: "Wisdom has built her house; she has carved its seven columns" (Prov. 9:1).

James specifically describes the seven pillars: purity, peaceable, gentle, yielding, merciful, humble, and sincere.

But the wisdom from above is first of all pure. It is also peace loving, gentle at all times, and willing to yield to

*others. It is full of mercy and the fruit of good deeds. It
shows no favoritism and is always sincere.*
—James 3:17

Per Alpha International's website *Bible in One Year*, there are seven steps to obtain wisdom. I'll use this example as it fits well within law enforcement parameters.

1. Handling Criticism

When insulted or verbally abused, don't respond in kind. This will only inflame the person whom you are dealing with and create an unnecessary officer safety situation.

> *Whoever corrects a mocker invites insults; whoever re-
> bukes the wicked incurs abuse. Do not rebuke mockers
> or they will hate you; rebuke the wise and they will love
> you. Instruct the wise and they will be wiser still; teach
> the righteous and they will add to their learning.*

> *The fear of the Lord is the beginning of wisdom, and
> knowledge of the Holy One is understanding. For
> through wisdom your days will be many, and years will
> be added to your life. If you are wise, your wisdom will
> reward you; if you are a mocker, you alone will suffer.*
> —Proverbs 9:7–12

As I've written a few times throughout this book, if we are insulted, we must let it go. Wisdom is gained by fearing (respecting and following) the Father with the knowledge of understanding gained from the Holy One, Jesus!

2.   Responding to Suffering

Jesus's response to those suffering always compassion.

- Healing the grief of a mother whose only son had died: "When the Lord saw her, He felt compassion for her, and said to her, 'Do not weep!'" (Luke 7:13).

- The woman who had been bleeding for twelve years: "Jesus turned around and saw her, and said, 'Courage, daughter! Your faith has saved you.' And from that hour the woman was cured" (Matt. 9:22).

As we often deal with people at their worst, either physically or emotionally, we need to compassion toward others, both as law enforcement officers and as Christians.

This section also deals with how we react when bad things happen to us for no reason. The Lord uses these instances to see how we will react when we suffer unfairly or unjustly. In Acts 5, the apostles were overjoyed to have beaten unjustly by the Sanhedrin for proclaiming eternal life through Jesus. In his letters, Paul describes the sufferings that endured for preaching about Christ:

> But even if you suffer for doing what is right, God will reward you for it. So, don't worry or be afraid of their threats. (1 Pet. 3:14)

> Yes, and everyone who wants to live a godly life in Christ Jesus will suffer persecution. (2 Tim. 3:12)

Jesus said that we would endure suffering on his behalf if we choose to follow him:

And I will show him how much he must suffer for my name's sake. (Acts 9:16)

Then Jesus said to his disciples, "If any of you wants to be my follower, you must turn from your selfish ways, take up your cross, and follow me. If you try to hang on to your life, you will lose it. But if you give up your life for my sake, you will save it." (Matt. 16:24–25)

People throughout the world are still persecuted and suffer unjustly for their love of God, often losing their lives for their faith. Christians in Asia must conduct their worship services in secret. Jews during the Holocaust were nearly eliminated because of their love of God. Jews and Christians are still imprisoned in certain countries because of their faith.

Today in America, Christians are being slandered and ridiculed because of our faith in Jesus. In what was a country based upon the freedom to worship God, Satan has used this freedom to trick many in America into believing that freedom means we can do whatever we want. This type of sinful freedom has crept into our governing officials, laws, and media. It has impacted our children, education, and our faith.

But evil people and impostors will flourish. They will deceive others and will themselves be deceived.
—2 Timothy 3:13

Be still in the presence of the Lord, and wait patiently for him to act. Don't worry about evil people who prosper or fret about their wicked schemes. Stop being angry! Turn from your rage! Do not lose your temper— it only leads to harm. For the wicked will be destroyed, but those who trust in the Lord will possess the land.

Soon the wicked will disappear. Though you look for them, they will be gone. The lowly will possess the land and will live in peace and prosperity.
—Psalm 37:7–11

3.   Pruning and Planting

The website lists this section as creating ministries or in-depth Christian relationships for salvation, citing the parables of the fig tree, mustard seed, and yeast in Luke 13. As we rarely have this opportunity, We can use the parable of the mustard seed to show that if we conduct ourselves as followers of Christ, we can impact others in our short time with them.

I would also suggest the parable of the sower in Matthew 13:1–23. When Jesus mentions anyone who hears the Word and understands it, I believe that our actions when dealing with the public and peers can allow them to "hear" the Word.

I've had people that I either had arrested, or were inmates while I worked the jail, ask me if I was a Christian. Of course, I said yes. With few exceptions, I did not speak to them about our Savior. It was Jesus working through me via my actions that led them to this conclusion.

War Stories

I was working day shift and received a call of a naked suicidal man. Upon arriving, I met his girlfriend (the informant). She told me that he had lost everything in the stock market and wanted to kill himself. Her boyfriend (the subject) was in the front yard: a 6'2" man about two hundred pounds and naked as a jaybird. He told me that he was junk and was worthless. He had lost everything.

I asked him if he believed in God. He said yes. I asked him if God had made him. He said yes. I asked if God made junk. He said no. Then I told him, "You must not be junk." He immediately jumped into my arms and said, "You're my guardian angel!"

As I held him, I had one thigh one my left forearm and one thigh one my right forearm. You can imagine what was pressed against my chest. After a few seconds, he let go. His entire attitude had changed, and he was now positive. His girlfriend was ecstatic that he was no longer suicidal.

I was only at the call for about twenty minutes, yet his entire outlook on life had changed. I bring this incident up to show how God uses us to help others. By the way, it took about three months of good-natured ribbing from the station as a "guardian angel" because of the naked man. I was thrilled that the Lord chose me to help this man out of a dire situation.

4. Knowing When to Confront

Jesus knew when to confront. He responded to confrontation; he did not initiate it. His response ranged from a calm response to physical confrontation, depending on the situation.

> Pharisees:
> Woe to you, scribes and Pharisees, hypocrites! For you are like whitewashed tombs which on the outside appear beautiful, but inside they are full of dead men's bones and all uncleanness. So, you too, outwardly appear righteous to men, but inwardly you are full of hypocrisy and lawlessness. (Matt. 23:27–28)

> Money changers:
> In the temple he found those who were selling oxen and sheep and pigeons, and the money-changers sitting there. And making a whip of cords, he drove them all out of the temple, with the sheep and oxen. And he poured out the coins of the money-changers and overturned their tables. And he told those who sold the pigeons, "Take these things away; do not make my Father's house a house of trade." (John 2:13–16)

> Jesus in the temple at age twelve:
> His parents didn't know what to think. "Son," his mother said to him, "why have you done this to us? Your father and I have been frantic, searching for you everywhere."

"But why did you need to search?" he asked. "Didn't you know that I must be in my Father's house?" (Luke 2:48–49)

Knowing when to confront requires both wisdom from the Father and knowledge (understanding) from the Son. As law enforcement officers, we react to a situation; we don't initiate. In most instances, we let others dictate how a situation will be handled. If a person is totally cooperative, then the situation is handled calmly with no need for any escalation of force. However, if a person is verbally abusive or is perceived as a threat, our senses become more acute, and we deal with the person more cautiously. If the person becomes physically aggressive, then we must escalate in our approach to them.

This is why we often see critical incidents in slow motion. The Lord gave us this ability to help us think on our feet and make good split-second decisions. Remember, blessed are the peacemakers, not blessed are the punching bags!

5. Turning to Jesus

We all err, sin, and do not pass every trial, especially given some of the stressful and horrendous situations that we handle. However, by confessing our sins and truly repenting, we continue to trust in God through faith in Jesus.

> *I will say to the Lord, "My refuge and my fortress, my God, in whom I trust." For he will deliver you from the snare of the fowler and from the deadly pestilence. He will cover you with his pinions, and under his wings you will find refuge; his faithfulness is a shield and buckler. You will not fear the terror of the night, nor the arrow that flies by day, nor the pestilence that stalks in darkness, nor the destruction that wastes at noonday.*
> *—Psalms 91:2–6*

> *If we confess our sins, he is faithful and just to forgive*
> *us our sins and to cleanse us from all unrighteousness.*
> —1 John 1:9

> *But, as it is written, "What no eye has seen, nor ear*
> *heard, nor the heart of man imagined, what God has*
> *prepared for those who love him."*
> —1 Corinthians 2:9

> *The Lord is faithful, who will establish you and guard*
> *you from the evil one.*
> —2 Thessalonians 3:3

6.　Testing Prophecy

This can be interpreted in two different ways. The first would be to test what is spoken by teachers, pastors, evangelists, and preachers.

> *Beloved, do not believe every spirit, but test the spirits*
> *to see whether they are from God, because many false*
> *prophets have gone out into the world.*
> —1 John 4:1

> *Now these were more noble-minded than those in*
> *Thessalonica, for they received the word with great ea-*
> *gerness, examining the Scriptures daily to see whether*
> *these things were so.*
> —Acts 17:11

The second interpretation would be how we carry out orders and directives that test our Christian faith. This is another tough trial, as often we are directed to complete tasks that go against what God wants us to do.

Supervisors often direct us with their own personal gain in mind. This could be to gain a promotion, win favor with their supervisors or city fathers, or act out of hate. Subordinate officers who either fear them or want to be accepted into the supervisor's clique for their personal gain will usually not challenge the supervisor's unethical behavior.

I've known a few officers who refused to oppose a supervisor's illegal or unethical directive. In one instance, seven officers went to prison—including the supervisor. In another, four officers went to prison, but the supervisors did not. While going to prison is the rarity, more common are instances when we are asked to change data or embellish a report to ensure a filing.

I know that it is hard to deny an order, but we must stay true to the Lord. I was kicked out of great job I had because I would not modify data on a report that I had written. As a result, it took me nineteen years to be promoted from sergeant to lieutenant. I was advised by my division chief that I had to "find a new home" because I could not be trusted. I told him that I answered to a much higher authority than the sheriff. He didn't know what to say.

> *Peter and the other Apostles replied: "We must obey*
> *God rather than human beings!"*
> —Acts 5:29

7. Revering God

It takes great perseverance and patience to become a law enforcement officer. It is not simply a job, but a career or a calling. Throughout the Bible, God has shown his love of peacekeepers and justice—which is what law enforcement is all about. As Christians, we believe that God places us in specific situations for a specific purpose, which we may never learn.

> *Now God has us where he wants us, with all the time in*
> *this world and the next to shower grace and kindness*
> *upon us in Christ Jesus. Saving is all his idea, and all*
> *his work. All we do is trust him enough to let him do*

it. It's God's gift from start to finish! We don't play the major role.
—Ephesians 2:10

For you are a people holy to the Lord your God. The Lord your God has chosen you to be a people for his treasured possession, out of all the peoples who are on the face of the earth.
—Deuteronomy 7:6

Knowing this, we should be eternally grateful that he called us for this special purpose. We are provided numerous opportunities to evangelize every day through words and actions: "Therefore, my brothers and sisters, make every effort to confirm your calling and election. For if you do these things, you will never stumble" (2 Pet. 1:10).

To gain the powerful gift of wisdom as described above, you can use prior life experiences with a Christian perspective or ask the Lord directly for wisdom. When you ask the Lord, you must ask with an earnest heart and truly believe.

Working with the public can be difficult at times, no matter what your profession. Before I joined the LASD, I worked at McDonald's in high school and then Thrifty Drug Stores in college (home of the *best* ice cream). I was young, and my patience was at an all-time high, yet there were some people who could not be pleased, no matter what I did for them. If these people received a check for a million dollars, they would complain that the signature was sloppy. I knew better that to respond in kind to these trials, as I did not want to lose my job. I would take a deep breath, say to myself, "Give me strength, Lord!" and then wait on them. It didn't always work, but more times than not, it did. I learned to read people. As I got older, I realized that this gift given to me was one of wisdom and was invaluable.

To list each reason why people are difficult would fill many books, but take the time to look at and listen to people when you deal with them. You would be surprised how much you learn and the knowledge you gain when dealing with similar behavior in the future. Difficult people will literally test your faith. I know it may sound weird, but try to use these situations to demonstrate your faith through actions. Most of these trials can be handled successfully by speaking with the person. Try not to take the person's actions personally.

At times, I have been called everything but a gentleman. When I was a young deputy on the streets or working in the jails, I found it more difficult to let go being called a pig, told to have sex with myself, or having someone suck their teeth. I'm truly glad that had enough faith (and wisdom—thank you, Lord!) not to handle these situations as "street justice."

As human beings, we are imperfect, and we all have weaknesses and frailties; 2 Corinthians 12:10 states, "When I am weak, then I am strong." This means that we are in control of our weakness, and the Lord is controlling our lives. The Lord cannot control your life unless you totally submit to Jesus. When you submit to Jesus, you want to live as he did.

For this very reason, make every effort to add to your faith goodness; and to goodness, knowledge; and to knowledge, self-control; and to self-control, perseverance; and to perseverance, godliness; and to godliness, mutual affection; and to mutual affection, love. For if you possess these qualities in increasing measure, they will keep you from being ineffective and unproductive in your knowledge of our Lord Jesus Christ. But whoever does not have them is nearsighted and blind, forgetting that they have been cleansed from their past sins. Therefore, my brothers and sisters, make every effort to confirm your calling and election. For if you do these things, you will never stumble.
—2 Peter 1:5–10

Do not merely listen to the word, and so deceive yourselves. Do what it says. Anyone who listens to the word but does not do what it says is like someone who looks

> *at his face in a mirror and, after looking at himself,*
> *goes away and immediately forgets what he looks like.*
> *But whoever looks intently into the perfect law that*
> *gives freedom, and continues in it—not forgetting what*
> *they have heard, but doing it—they will be blessed in*
> *what they do.*
> —James 1:22–25

We don't have all the answers in handling our duties. Only one person can be all things, to all people, at all times—and it is not any of us! As I was told in the academy, "There are several ways to skin a cat." A prayer that I said every day before I got into my radio car was this: "Lord give the strength and wisdom to deal with what is going to happen today. Let me treat everyone the same way I want to be treated."

That prayer of wisdom got me through a lot of situations. I was able to talk my way out of at least four shootings, numerous uses of force, and a plethora of citizen complaints. The Lord also provided me the wisdom to know when to use force and when to stop.

As mentioned earlier, we often have to make split-second decisions that could have a permanent impact on both the public and on us. We can be second-guessed by administration, the public, and the media for years over an incident that occurred in the blink of an eye. Wisdom is key in these situations.

War Stories

I was a new deputy, twenty-four years old and just off training for about a week. A call went out that there was a man under the influence of PCP in the street. In the 1980s, PCP users were almost as common as drunks, only a *lot* more violent and strong. A few minutes after the handling unit arrived, the dispatcher asked the handling unit to advise what was happening.   Neither the handling nor assisting unit responded.

I told the dispatcher that I was responding, but I did not state that I was responding Code 3- lights and sirens.

As I approached an intersection, I saw that traffic in all directions had stopped. However, as I entered the intersection, I saw a car in a left-turn lane pull around a car stopped in front of it and make the left turn. I swerved and hit the brakes but could not avoid the crash. I can still remember spinning my radio car 3.5 times before I wrapped it around a pole, as everything slowed. My vehicle, a 1981 Plymouth Grand Fury, had become the size of a VW Bug when I got out. I checked on the car that I hit. There was a pregnant mother and her nine-year-old son in the front passenger seat.

The mother was conscious and breathing, but her son was breathing and not conscious. The radio in my vehicle was dead, so I ran to the nearest business and called the station. The watch sergeant was able to interpret my rapid and highly excited speech and had paramedics respond. The mother and unborn baby survived. Her nine-year-old son did not. Additionally, the day before, I had learned that my ex-wife was pregnant with our first child. I was not allowed to contact the family nor apologize after the crash, although I wanted to very badly.

A few years later, after I transferred to another station, I received a loud party call. I spoke with the woman who answered when I knocked on the door. I advised her that we received a call that her music was too loud. I told her that the music didn't bother me, but it did her neighbors. I asked her to please turn the music down. She said that she would, and that I was very nice—not like the deputy who had killed her son a few years back.

After I got her name, I realized that she was the driver of the car that I had hit a few years earlier. I then saw a toddler walk up and stand next to her mom. I did not tell her that I was the deputy, but I apologized that she had lost a child. I got back in the radio car and advised my desk that I was responding to the station to advise the watch commander.

Although I had been hit with not just a wave of emotions, but a tsunami, I kept my cool. I did not exhibit any emotion until I got back into my radio car. Remember, at times we have to be the ultimate actors. I took a deep breath and thanked the Lord that he helped me handle the situation in a professional manner.

A split-second decision cost a family a son and resulted in about ten years of depression for me. I was filed on for vehicular manslaughter (rejected by the district attorney), suspended for twenty days, and sued by the family (the suit was dropped against me after my deposition).

I bet you are saying, "Where's the wisdom?"

At the time of the crash, and when I contacted the mother a few years later, my walk with the Lord was very weak. However, I never stopped revering God and acknowledging that Jesus is the Messiah. Although it took me ten years to get past the traffic accident and forgive myself, the Lord came through in his time—not mine. He did not forsake me.

I believe that there was a reason for that crash and the years of guilt. I may never know the reason, but I was able to impart lessons that had I learned through this and other incidents throughout my career to the hundreds of LASD employees that I would eventually either work with or supervise over my thirty-two years in law enforcement.

I gave the Lord credit for the good incidents that I was involved in, and rightfully so, as he placed me in the LASD for a reason. Yet I never blamed the Lord for the negative or emotionally charged events. These were trials, not tests, as the Lord does not test us. He provides us strength to handle any situation we come up against, if we truly believe. This was a lesson that I did not fully understand when I became a deputy sheriff at twenty-two, but I learned, through his wisdom, as I progressed throughout my career.

About the Author

Bob Blanks is a retired lieutenant with the Los Angeles County Sheriff's Department. In his thirty-two years of law enforcement service, he worked custody, patrol, courts, and gangs, both as a frontline deputy and as a supervisor. He is married with three children, three stepchildren, and four grandchildren. In addition to spending as much time with the grandkids as possible, he enjoys running, gardening, and canning.

Although he was raised as a Christian, he accepted the Lord at age thirty-two, when he went through both a divorce and a promotion to an assignment 80 miles from his home. The combination of divorce, not seeing his children every day, and driving 160 miles a day was the low point in his life. However, the Lord never left him; he helped him through his trials and transformed his life.

Endnotes

1   McCoy, Shawn & Aamodt, Michael. (2010). A Comparison of Law Enforcement Divorce Rates with Those of Other Occupations. Journal of Police and Criminal Psychology. 25. 1-16. 10.1007/s11896-009-9057-8.

2   Police On-Duty Drug Use: A Theoretical and Descriptive Examination – Kraska, Kapeller. On the Front Lines – Hepp. Violanti, JM, Fekedulegn D, Charles LE, Andrew ME, Hartley TA, Mnatsakanova A, Burchfield CM (2009). Suicide in Police Work: Exploring Potential Contributing Influences. American Journal of Criminal Justice, 34, 41-53. Violanti JM (2010). Police suicide: A national comparison with fire-fighter and military personnel. International Journal of Police Strategies & Management, 33, 270-286. DOI 10.1108/13639511011044885. Carlier IV, Lamberts RD and Gersons BP. (1997). Risk factors for posttraumatic stress symptomology in police officers: A prospective analysis. Journal of Nervous and Mental Disorders, 185, 498-506. Gersons BP. (1989). Patterns of PTSD among police officers following shooting incidents: A two-dimensional model and treatment implications. Journal of Traumatic Stress, 2, 247-257. Ibid.

3   https://www.therecoveryvillage.com/alcohol-abuse/related-topics/facts-alcoholism-police-officers/

4   https://www.officer.com/training-careers/article/12156622/2015-police-suicide-statistics
https://bluehelp.org/
 https://www.fbi.gov/news/pressrel/press-releases/fbi-releases

5   https://rudermanfoundation.org/white_papers/police-officers-and-firefighters-are-more-likely-to-die-by-suicide-than-in-line-of-duty/

6   https://www.fbi.gov/news/pressrel/press-releases/fbi-releases

7   Violanti JM, Gu JK, Charles LE, Fekedulegn D, Andrew ME, Burchfiel CM. Is suicide higher among separated/retired police officers? an epidemiological investigation. *Int J Emerg Ment Health*. 2011;13(4):221-228.

8   Los Angeles County Sheriff's Department 2019 Year in Review

9   https://post.ca.gov/peace-officer-candidate-selection-standards